# Goodbye to
# MUM
## and
# DAD

Taking Stock of the Past Year

ANDREW KIRBY-PUGH

**author**HOUSE®

*AuthorHouse™ UK*
*1663 Liberty Drive*
*Bloomington, IN 47403 USA*
*www.authorhouse.co.uk*
*Phone: UK TFN: 0800 0148641 (Toll Free inside the UK)*
*        UK Local: 02036 956322 (+44 20 3695 6322 from outside the UK)*

*Published by AuthorHouse 10/14/2020*

*ISBN: 978-1-6655-8064-9 (sc)*
*ISBN: 978-1-6655-8065-6 (hc)*
*ISBN: 978-1-6655-8063-2 (e)*

# Contents

# *Preface*

Until recently I never had any ambition or intention to produce a book of any sort and certainly hadn't been motivated to write a family history or memoir. I was aware that writing was something I could do quite well, though, as over the years I had scripted articles, magazine contributions, work proposals, and even the occasional poem or play. At school and college, I happily embarked on essays and dissertations, and I generally received good scores. Even in the days of frequent letter writing, I enjoyed putting pen to paper, and my efforts seemed to be well received.

But what follows hadn't been planned. However, changing circumstances and events in my life over the past year, and coping with the loss of both my parents in the space of less than five months, has brought a different perspective. As I dealt with things and faced my emotions and personal loss, alongside the obvious practicalities I found myself reflecting more and more, remembering the past and how important my parents had been to me. We had always been a close family of three, and I valued their opinions in matters of finance and career to the end. We probably didn't talk too much about relationships and personal matters, but I don't think sons necessarily do, and it didn't affect the bond between us as a family.

As events progressed over the year, I took great comfort in talking to family and friends, sharing worries and concerns and, of course more recently, stories and memories. However, once things began to settle, albeit in a different way, I had a growing sense that I should do something more than just talk to those who were kind enough to listen. And so one Monday morning, I sat down and started to write, and I didn't stop for a week. This is the result. What follows is a ramble, a mix of family memories, thoughts, and feelings as they came to me, and an account of events as they happened over the year. I didn't research. Everything is as told to or experienced by me. Most of the family background was known to those who knew Mum and Dad, but there are also stories here which were told to me directly or were experienced by just the three of us.

I didn't tell anyone I was writing anything until I had finished, mainly because I didn't know what I would include, who would be mentioned, or what the result would be. I didn't have an audience in mind, but I hope people, not just family and friends, will want to read it now that's it's finished. It probably doesn't convey everything I thought, or think, of Mum and Dad. That's not something I have found easy to put into words. As a result, it might come across as too factual in places and doesn't pay them enough respect or fully express my love. But it's genuine, and I think my voice comes through.

Once finished, I did ask our good friend Geraldine, mentioned throughout, to read it as she knew Mum and Dad well and helped me a lot throughout the year. I am grateful for her comments and embellishments which have all been incorporated. I have subsequently let everyone who is mentioned know that I've produced it. Without exception, all have been supportive, and I hope they might come round to reading it. Above all, I have to thank Nolan, who let me disappear to my study and work at it. He encouraged me throughout and also took time to read the final updated version, giving advice and feedback which I have valued tremendously.

April 2020

# Family Trees

# THE PUGH FAMILY

**Reginald Pugh *m* Edith Morgan**

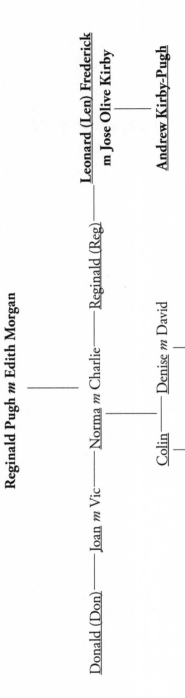

Donald (Don) —— Joan *m* Vic —— Norma *m* Charlie —— Reginald (Reg) —— **Leonard (Len) Frederick**
**m Jose Olive Kirby**

Colin —— Denise *m* David

**Andrew Kirby-Pugh**

# THE KIRBY FAMILY

**Herbert Kirby m Edith (Edie) Feast**

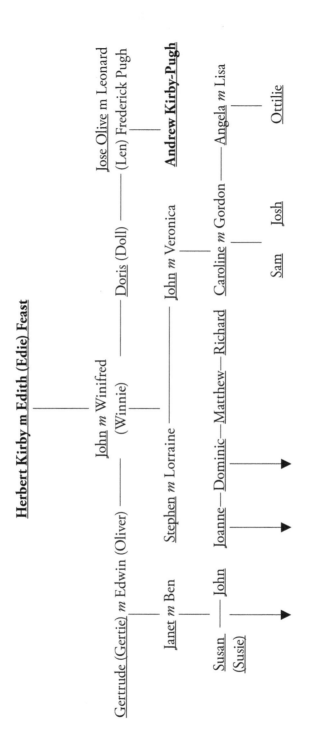

# Chapter 1

## MY FAMILY

Yesterday, on his first birthday, Frankie went into the sea for the first time. Happy, playful, inquisitive, and full of energy, everything one could hope for in a healthy puppy. A year ago he was just being born, and I was nowhere near the sea.

Until February last year, my immediate family life had been following the same routine and patterns. Mum, Dad, and I were comfortable to a degree—certainly I was—and whilst things weren't dull or uneventful exactly, all seemed relatively predictable, with the three of us no doubt subconsciously preparing for the changes we knew would come in the not-too-distant future.

I was living happily with Nolan in our two-year-old new build in Hackney Wick, overlooking the canal close to the Olympic Stadium. My parents, Jose and Len, were in the family home in Winchmore Hill, which they had bought for £9,000 in 1969. Our new apartment was modern in style, with a few carefully chosen or inherited antique pieces. It was a good, clean, easily manageable London base for the years ahead. We had chosen it because of its easy train and road access to Deal in Kent, where we planned to acquire a seaside home once I retired.

1

Mum and Dad, after fifty years in residence, were still able to take pride in their 1930s three-bedroom semi in The Spinney, a respectable, family-friendly suburb. A well-appointed garden overlooked a bank of trees screening off the properties beyond. Mum loved her garden, although lamented the heavy clay. Over time, she had spent considerable effort cultivating a variety of shrubs and plants that constantly drew admiration from friends and neighbours. Of particular pride were her large acer, taking the space once occupied by my garden swing, and the yellowish-green 'Welsh tree' which they had brought back from a family holiday in Solva ages ago. How that had grown over the years! It was a challenge for Darren, the gardener, to trim each spring, but it was certainly stunning to see at the rear end of the lawn in front of the fence. Dad enjoyed gardening, too, but took my mother's lead, although he was in charge of grass mowing and watering. The two of us were responsible for painting the garage which extended into the garden from the drive on the side, and for creosoting wooden fencing when required. Although willing to give things a try, Dad was not very good at DIY or home improvement, but Mum loved seeing us work together, and he always helped me with decorating and repairs to my own properties. It was Mum who reigned over the house and garden, though, and made it what it was, keeping things going when times were economically restricting.

Over the years, Mum and Dad had made good friends in The Spinney—Katie and Dickie, Fionulla and Andy, Jill—and had many other good neighbours, although in the fifty years Mum and Dad had been there, the turnover, particularly in the house immediately next door, was pretty constant.

I was fortunate and appreciative to still have that home base after all those years, even though I hadn't lived there since returning from college in the early eighties. And for Mum and Dad to still be together after almost sixty-three years of marriage was, in the bigger scheme of things, quite remarkable. They actually first met and started "courting"—an old-fashioned term but one I think still carries a certain romanticism—seventy-one years ago. Dad, a keen and regular rower on the River Lee, started frequenting The Woodman, the nearby pub in Clapton, owned and run by my mother's parents, Herbert and Edith (Edie) Kirby. I don't think Mum actually pulled any pints, although she could, but she lived there, and the relationship started. Apparently after the first week, Dad told Mum he wouldn't see her again as, 'My mates will be back from holiday, and we tend to drink more locally in Homerton.' But Mum obviously had *something*, and Dad went back for more. They didn't rush things. They went out for four years and were engaged a further four before marrying in 1956. I didn't come along for yet another four.

Mum, and Dad too, often said that his family, the Pughs, thought Dad had, 'married above his station', although Mum was certainly not disliked or resented. Both came from large families, although circumstances were socially different. The Kirbys came from a long line of business entrepreneurs, with Herbert and Edie owning a number of pubs in the East End and down in Southend and Leigh-on-Sea, The Spreadeagle in Shoreditch among them. Cousin Stephen, my uncle John's oldest son, has researched the maternal family tree, tracing us back centuries to the early Huguenots, arriving in the East End from France, through shopkeepers, cheesemakers, cloth merchants, publicans, and with some connection apparently to Lockwood's, the canning business. All entrepreneurial trade in one way or another. Some of the ancestor lines have proved a little hazy, with a sprinkling of illegitimacy, possibly bigamy and petty crime, but a rich pedigree, and one the Kirbys have always delighted in. Well apart from Auntie Gertie, Mum's oldest sister, who was wonderful, artistic, funny, slightly eccentric, but undoubtedly a snob when it came to the East End history. It was said of Gertie in her younger days that she looked like the British film star Jessie Matthews, and she did, but she hated the reference.

Mum was the youngest of four; Gertrude (Gertie) was the eldest, followed by Uncle John and Auntie Doris, known as Doll. The name John has appeared in most generations of Mum's family. During the great fire of London, Samuel Pepys took refuge with a John Kirby at Kirby's Castle in Bethnal Green, on the site of what is now the Toy Museum. At the time of the fire, Bethnal Green was just outside London. This John Kirby was a wealthy silk merchant, and I like to think, despite the fact that no great wealth has ever passed down, he was an ancestor of ours, developing the Huguenots' talents for cloth manufacture. Mum told the story that once she was on a bus with Cousin Stephen going past the site, and Stephen announced, 'That's where we come from.' Given the site had once housed a lunatic asylum and the John Kirby story had yet to emerge, Mum was not amused. But whatever Stephen's young knowledge might have been—and he was well-educated and steeped in history—his comment was typical of his enduring sense of cheek and anecdote.

Dad was born not far from Clapton in Homerton, a poorer district then. He lived with his parents, Reginald and Edith Pugh, in a tenement along with his brothers and sisters, Donald (Don), Reginald (Reg), Joan, and Norma. Dad was named Leonard Frederick. The family wasn't rich, but Dad's memories are happy. In his stories to me in later life, he delighted in telling me he was the favourite child, particularly with neighbours and the wider family, who used to spoil him with trips to the Hackney Empire followed by pie and eel shops. Always an active sportsman—rowing, diving, and swimming particularly—he also went regularly to the long-gone sports stadium near to home. Hackney Marshes were close to hand for football. Dad did not have a great education, but he was bright and clever in his way. Although he liked to read and devoured newspapers daily, he retained an academic ignorance resulting from a lack of formal, advanced educational opportunities. However, he was bright enough at the school he did attend to win a scholarship to a notable school where pupils were dressed in knickerbockers apparently. However, his parents would not allow him to go as his siblings had not had the same opportunity, and in this case at least, they did not want to show favouritism. Noble but regrettable. Dad was expected to go out to work instead to help support the family, which he did, but he bettered himself along the way, taking elocution lessons to help his prospects. With brother Reg following close behind, Dad became a successful stockbroker for Casenove's in the City before redundancy hit in the 1960s. He then worked as an accountant for the Midland Bank at their Princes Street office opposite the Bank of England for the remainder of his career before redundancy unfortunately hit again. I have my father's office chair from the bank by my desk at home. I know he didn't receive much of a settlement when his job was made redundant, but at least he got a fine chair.

Dad used to have to visit the Bank of England during the course of his duties, and one day he arrived home with a bandaged hand; he'd caught his index finger in the heavy old Bank of England doors. His finger was bent rigid from then on.

During the time he was at the bank, I used to produce a weekly magazine, all handwritten with pasted pictures and photos, called *It's Hear and Now.* It was a bit of fun, produced for me as much as for the select group of family and friends who bought a copy. Every week, Dad took the master to work and photocopied enough copies for me to sell, something which I know he shouldn't have done, but he always supported me.

Mum and Dad often shared memories of their early times in the East End with me, and I can also dimly remember sights that hinted at what life must have been like in Clapton and Homerton at that time. Members of both Kirbys and Pughs remained in the area for many years after Mum and Dad had leapt at the chance to move further north to commuting suburbia, so we made frequent family visits back. Dad recalled travelling upfront on the old steam locomotive that ran along the route of today's overground and pitching a ride on the horse-drawn milk cart. I'm not sure which school he did attend, but contemporaries there included the Beverley Sisters, the glamorous and successful 1950s singing trio. Apparently they were twins and an older cousin, Joy, rather than the three actual sisters they constantly sang about. Joy married a footballer and then lived quite near Mum and Dad in North London. They frequently saw her at their local nursery in Enfield. Dad never hesitated to remind her of their old East End beginnings and school, which I understand she acknowledged and also remembered with affection.

Mum's childhood was more comfortable. Although "trade", the Kirbys also owned property in Essex, and the houses surrounding their home at The Woodman pub in Clapton were large and genteel. That changed in the war, when many of these were bombed, to be replaced later by vast, uniform blocks of flats. But I can remember as a very young child seeing large derelict buildings with the outline of neglected tennis courts and gardens dotted along Springfield, the road where Auntie Doll was living when we visited, just up the hill from the pub. And Springfield Park itself, with its boating lake, bowling green, and well-tendered flower beds and lawns leading down the steep hill to the River Lee, gave an indication of better town planning and more indulgent times.

Mum was an Essex girl, born on 18 April 1928 in Ilford, where Herbert and Edie lived, running their pubs remotely. I don't think they had The Woodman then, but it couldn't have been much long after as Mum lived there from quite an early age. Mum was a late addition; Gertie, John, and Doll were no longer children, and I think both Gertie and John were already married when Mum came along, Gertie to Edwin (known as Oliver) and John to Winifred (known as Winnie). Auntie Doll was certainly in her early twenties. When I was born, she took on the role of surrogate grandmother to me. All the family adored Auntie Doll, and today, my cousin Caroline is her spitting image. In 1928, Herbert wasn't in good health, so Evie's pregnancy was certainly a miracle and most likely a shock. Apparently Doll thought Herbert, her dad, was 'disgusting' for having done the deed, and Edie took to jumping off the kitchen table and bathing in gin, so horrified was she to be expecting another baby at a relatively late age. However, when Mum arrived, she was adored and spoiled rotten, despite the social stigma perceived, and maybe experienced, by Edie. When passing neighbours or customers while walking down the street with baby Mum, Edie used to quickly hand her to Auntie Doll. 'Pretend she's yours, pretend she's yours!' Mum said, illegitimacy supposedly being more acceptable than late motherhood. And the story goes that Doll was sent off to register the birth with the words, 'Oh, call her what you like', but this wasn't true. The names Jose Olive had been chosen and agreed to by both parents.

After Auntie Doll died, we found her wartime ration book, which gave her date of birth, showing she was a year older than we and she thought. We'd celebrated her eightieth birthday when she was actually eighty-one. Mum missed Auntie Doll very much after she died. Not only was she my surrogate grandmother but she had in effect become Mum's surrogate mother.

Mum never thought of herself as pretty or attractive, although photos I have suggest otherwise. In early pictures, she had short, bobbed, blondish, straight hair. She looks to have been healthy and happy, whether on the beach in a fully dressed, suited, and booted family group, or leaning on farming equipment in fields, probably just the Marshes, with her dad. Things changed, though, when she was consigned to bed with a bad case of rheumatic fever for a number of months. She recovered completely, although she was convinced her swollen ankles in later life were the result of the infection. Mum played a lot of tennis and cycled but could never swim. She was skilled at table tennis and was a sharp darts player. In my teens, when I had tennis lessons in Winchmore Hill, the coach turned out to be an old coach of my mother's; we could only guess his age. She once cycled from London to Southend, but only the once. To get to her first job, at Elizabeth Arden's in Ealing, she frequently cycled rather than take the long and arduous public transport trip from Clapton. She met Miss Arden once, when the latter came on a visit, and Mum remained a loyal and passionate devotee of Arden products, notably their Eight Hour Cream.

School for Mum was initially at a convent in nearby Stamford Hill, although we're not Catholic. As sister Gertie had produced a daughter herself shortly after Mum was born, my cousin Janet, the two girls found themselves at school together and in the same class. Mum recalled being addressed by Janet as 'Auntie' at school, something she didn't appreciate at all.

Mum's closest friend when young was Joy, and they did everything and went everywhere together. After Joy met a New Zealander, Bob, and moved back there to marry and settle and raise a family, they kept in regular contact. In 1976, Joy and Bob came over for a visit. Mum and Dad and I went to meet them at Paddington Station. Mum was so excited to see her again, and I remember her running down the platform to greet her. In the weeks that followed, Mum and Joy chatted and laughed away like teenagers. It was a different side to my mother, one I hadn't witnessed before, and it was lovely to see.

Mum adored and worshipped her parents, Herbert and Edie, as did Doll and her brother, John. I've a lovely photograph of Herbert and Doll taking a stroll arm in arm along a promenade. Herbert worked hard, despite being in poor health, but it seems it was Edie who had the business mind. A determined and headstrong woman, she was, by all accounts, also kind, compassionate, and totally supportive of her family. When John's wartime call-up papers arrived, she tore them up. She was fiercely patriotic, but her son wasn't going anywhere. He did, of course, and was conscripted to the navy, luckily having a "good" war without too many incidents. Herbert was too old or infirm to be called up for the war, but both did their bits at home. The pub remained open, supporting loyal and remaining customers and businessmen, a diverse ethnic group of people even in those days. Steven knows of a story where Edie helped defend a nearby Jewish shop from attack and looting. Inside had been the owner's pregnant wife. Stories also abound of the many colourful characters of the time, with names like Sonny Bloom. It was well known that some of them took advantage of trading loopholes during the hard, rationed wartime years.

Auntie Doll spent her last years in sheltered housing in Clapton, on the site of the church where Mum and Dad had been married. She was reunited with some of those old faces from the past who, like Doll, had never moved far from their old stomping grounds. Cousin Stephen has lots of family stories from the years spent at The Woodman, and, of course, he was there. What a great television series it would make with both the family and regulars providing lots of drama and humour. I believe one of Stephen and Lorraine's children has the old wooden Woodman pub sign. I hope so. The pub has long gone, replaced by residential flats now.

Dad's father, Reginald, too old to go off to fight himself, acted as an air-raid warden during the war, a dangerous job in the East End which saw considerable destruction. Both Mum and Dad were evacuated, Dad to the South Coast and Mum to the Vale of Evesham. Edie and Auntie Doll often went down to see Mum, and she had fond memories of her time there. Mum, Dad, and I went to visit once when we were nearby on holiday, and Mum said that it was all very much the same and as she had remembered it.

Although an astute businesswoman, Edie loved life and spent everything she earned. Like all the Kirby women, she liked fine clothes and accessories, as well as good food. She loved going to the theatre and cinema, often with Mum and Doll. She liked cartoons. With Edie, Mum saw all the big West End musicals of the time – *South Pacific* among them, although they left *Annie Get Your Gun* early as Auntie Doll couldn't take the noise of the gunfire. Mum never saw her favourite, Frank Sinatra, in concert, or Judy Garland, whom she adored (other than in the *Wizard of Oz* for some reason), but with Edie and Doll, she did get to see Danny Kaye, which Mum said was the best thing she ever saw. The family loved ice hockey and frequently went to Haringey Stadium to watch live matches. Edie particularly loved horse racing in the days when it really was a special occasion to go, an opportunity to put on the finery, chance your money, catch a glimpse of the royals, but above all, behave respectfully.

Mum's brother John and his wife, Winnie, went on to have two sons, my cousins Stephen and John—yes, another John. Young John spent his life riding, grooming, and surrounding himself with horses and equestrian things, alongside running the family business with Uncle John, his father, so Grandma Edie obviously started something. The interest continues with John's eldest daughter, Caroline, a keen rider herself from an early age. Cousin John's second daughter, Angela, doesn't have much of an interest in horses but developed sporting prowess in other directions.

Edie also took the family on foreign cruises, something that was relatively rare in the late forties and fifties. But if she'd earned the money, she wanted to spend and enjoy it. I've inherited that streak.

Being elderly and in poor health, Herbert died when my mother was relatively young, and I'm not sure whether my Dad ever met him. I think it's unlikely, but Dad certainly met Edie and was embraced completely into the Kirby family, accompanying them on numerous trips and foreign cruises. Joining the family, with an array of strong-minded, highly sociable, and individualistic individuals, must have been daunting. When Cousin (Young) John married his wife, Veronica, she and Dad often sided together to joke about the clan they'd both taken on. Dad and Veronica were close and had a great affection for one another. After Cousin John died at only sixty-eight, both Mum and Dad were so pleased Veronica had the bravery to move on and find happiness in a totally new direction, meeting Bill from Australia and enjoying catching up on all those missed travel opportunities and holidays never taken with John.

Cousin John played a big part in Mum and Dad's courting. I was regularly reminded how John, then a teenager, accompanied them on their dates, such as on a trip to see *High Society*. I'm not sure if he was a chaperone or they were caretaking, as his parents, John and Winnie, were helping to run The Woodman by then.

When John was dating Veronica in the early sixties and the pub family had moved from Clapton to open a grocery shop, Kirbys of Crowthorne in Berkshire, I remember waiting at the window for John and Veronica to arrive each Sunday afternoon on their way back from going over the books in Loughton with Gertie's husband, Uncle Oliver. Photographs back up my memories of them as a very stylish and fashionable couple. Why do I remember Veronica in capri pants? I adored them, as did Mum and Dad, and we remained close as their family grew. Cousin John was one of my godfathers, and I'm godfather to his eldest daughter, Caroline, and her youngest son, Josh.

After eight years together, Mum and Dad finally married in Clapton on 4 April 1956. Apparently it snowed. After the ceremony at St Andrews Church, photos were taken at Auntie Gertie and Uncle Oliver's house in Loughton. Gertie's daughter (Mum's niece), Janet, was chief bridesmaid, and both full families were in attendance with one exception. Not long before the wedding, Grandma Edie had died. In the wedding photographs, whilst Dad looks full of pride and happiness, Mum appears sad but radiant. She was given away by her brother John. The reception was at the rambling King's Head pub in Chigwell.

Mum and Dad were a good match. Dad was highly sociable and could talk to anyone. Mum was naturally shy, unusual in the Kirby family, but she gained in confidence as she got older with Dad by her side. Mum covered up her shyness by talking a lot, and she said a lot of funny things. Dad was placid, with never a bad word to say about anyone. He hated confrontation. Mum was emotional at times, and I'm the same. Mum used to say the reason we argued was because we were so alike.

I don't know why it took four years of courting and four years of engagement before Mum and Dad eventually married. Maybe it was because Edie was unwell, or maybe it was financial. My parents were of the generation where you saved before you committed to anything that cost. Even Edie had done that. My parents never had credit cards until very late in life. And even then, Mum, who controlled the household finances with Dad providing the investment and stocks' and shares' knowledge, endeavoured to pay in full each month. The only exceptions were those massive mail-order catalogues with their weekly instalments that got passed around. I remember Marshall Ward and Kays.

Mum and Dad never really argued except over money, or lack of it. In the early sixties, Dad used to enjoy a not-infrequent bet on the pools and in the betting shop, which, coinciding with his first redundancy, brought quite dire money worries. I didn't really notice any hardship, but I know now how they needed to be bailed out by friends and family, but it all got paid back. From then on, with Dad working again, Mum took control of the household, something she did well. To help with the financial predicament, Mum took a

Saturday sales job in Enfield's Pearsons department store, and Dad work Sunday mornings in the Salisbury Pub in Winchmore Hill. In the seventies, when things were tight again, Dad took on a paper round for the *Enfield Advertiser*, and then a small job at a friend's laundry business in Barnet. Mum also used to get paid for testing or tasting new products. I remember her coming back one time having tasted frozen roast potatoes. 'Ridiculous', she said. 'They will never take off.'

From an early age, despite any failings on their part, Mum and Dad taught me the value of money and the importance of having the money first before spending. I was encouraged to sell toys through the local advertiser or by putting up cards in the newsagent's window. So I was able to save and buy my first portable cassette recorder and later, my Ferguson music centre.

If occasionally times were hard, I don't recall suffering or being hard done by. We had good, nourishing food, although now I realise we often had cheaper cuts of meat. Once Mum was furious when she caught me shovelling kidneys which I disliked into the old kitchen stove, which I'd seen her do with scraps. A waste of hard earned food, although I didn't get it at the time. We still had a car, although we did downsize from the family Ford Poplar Saloon to a smaller second-hand Ford Anglia, which horrified me at the time. Still, we had holidays with friends, mainly in Pembrokeshire, at Little Holland, and later in Broadstairs on the Kent coast. In 1966, during the school break, I went to stay with John and Veronica and their first dog, Tiny, in Berkshire. I know it was 1966 as Mum sent me a postcard marking the opening of the Post Office Tower. I might still have it. I also used to stay with Cousin Janet and her two children, John (another one!) and Suzie in their caravan in the New Forest, or more frequently, at Debden Green, near where Janet's mum, Auntie Gertie, lived. Looking back, the fact that I went away each year, often without Mum and Dad, was obviously of financial necessity. And even when we all went, there were sacrifices. Staying at Broadstairs once, Dad and I, with the friends we were with, took the Hovercraft one day from nearby Ramsgate to Zebrugge in Belgium without Mum. Publicly, Mum said she didn't want to go, but privately, it must have been an economic decision. Similarly, despite Mum's love of the cinema, I wasn't allowed to go with my school friends to Saturday morning pictures at the Southgate Odeon. But they did pay for me to have weekly riding lessons (one guinea) and spend a week each year doing stable management at Holly Hill Farm on the Ridgeway in Enfield. I went off that though after staying with Cousin John and helping him with the horses there, which were a lot less disciplined and docile.

Mum and Dad bought their first house when they married. They looked at North London, keen to get away from the East End, which wasn't going through the best of times, and settle in commuter land so that Dad could get to the City easily. They looked at Cockfosters first but settled on a small semi-detached in The Vale, Southgate, where they stayed for thirteen years before moving to the house in Winchmore Hill. Their adjoining neighbours were Jean and Norman Tripp and their daughters, Geraldine and Jennifer. Jean and Norman have been my parents' longest and best friends ever since. The Tripps have become a second family to us. Sadly, Norman is no longer with us, but Jean is, and at ninety-seven, she's now living and being cared for in a home near Geraldine. Jean is my godmother, and I am godfather to Geraldine's youngest, Vicky. Many holidays were taken with the Tripps. We stayed at Norman's sister's house in Little

Holland, and they introduced us to Pembrokeshire and Solva and St Davids. Both Jennifer and her husband, Gordon, and Geraldine and her husband, Richard, have homes in St Davids now.

Mum stayed at home to look after me before I was ready to go to school, a role not looked down on or criticised then. Sometimes Mum and I went down to Little Holland in the summer for a period, often with Auntie Doll, Gertie, Janet, Susie and John, Cousin John and Veronica, Stephen and Lorraine, and, of course, the Tripps. Dad used to come down straight from work on a Friday for the weekend. I have a vivid memory on being down on the beach with Mum and seeing Dad in his suit arrive on the cliffs above. Very happy times.

Apparently once, and I must have been under four, Mum and I were on the beach. A complete stranger approached and asked Mum if I would like to go out on his boat. Mum sent me off alone with him. Unthinkable now. I got back safely, unharmed.

I have lots of memories of us at Little Holland. Playing in the sea with Dad or donkey riding on the front. Plus trips to the amusements on the pier at Clacton. Endless days on the beach building sandcastles with Mum, sitting on an old upturned rowing boat with Auntie Doll. Walking to Kirby's Cross to get fresh cream in waxy paper pots decorated with hand-drawn cows. And always people coming and going. I remember one occasion when Lorraine got badly stung by a jellyfish.

There was a sizeable garden in The Vale. There was originally a pond, but it was subsequently filled in to prevent me from falling in. I was born in May 1960. The Tripps were there to greet us when Dad proudly drove Mum and I home from the hospital. Cradling me in her arms (no seatbelts then), the first thing Mum said to them was, 'What do I do with him?' But after that she did everything for me.

I've some lovely cine film footage (now on DVD) of Mum and I in the back garden in The Vale. Dad's hardly in shot; he was obviously filming. I've also got film of us all—and the Tripps and the Gibsons from across the street—out front, playing in very thick snow, Mum in her beloved sheepskin car coat. It was 1963–64, one of the worst winters on record. Jean can be spotted peering out of her front window, stuck inside with a blood clot in her leg, phlebitis. I look like Paddington with a duffle and wellington boots. My outfit of choice for when, a little while later, I decided to run away. I'd packed my small suitcase (a present from Cousin Janet; I still have it), but I didn't get beyond the porch. Mum wouldn't put my wellingtons on.

I remember lots of good things from our time in The Vale. Family visits obviously. As well as the Kirbys, Dad's brother Reg used to arrive in full leather on his motorbike. He never married and died tragically early in his fifties, dropping dead of a heart attack at the station on his way to work.

Dad used to amuse me by batting a cricket ball from the back garden over the roof into the road. But Mum soon told him off in case he hit anything, or indeed, anyone walking by. I can also see Dad sitting at the kitchen table, helping me paint and draw. I could never draw feet or shoes on people, and Dad used to draw them for me. In his way, he was probably quite artistic. Mum could never draw but always wished she could.

Music seemed to fill the house, either from the big wireless in the kitchen or the record-playing unit in the lounge, which could stack up to six albums or singles. I remember sitting on my dad's knee with Billy J. Kramer's *Little Children* playing. So the song, although not the greatest, has always meant something to me. Dad had eclectic taste. Along with Mum, he loved musicals and had the soundtracks to the shows they had seen, including Rex Harrison and Julie Andrews in *My Fair Lady*. Years later, once I was earning, I took them to see *Sweeny Todd*, *Crazy for You*, and *My Fair Lady* again, twice, once in London and then when I took them for a week's break in Edinburgh. My friend Trevor worked for Andrew Lloyd-Webber for a while and got me front row tickets to take Dad to see *Phantom of the Opera* at the Haymarket, which he really enjoyed. He also loved Mario Lanza, and I think had he received a better or fuller education, he would have had the confidence to embrace opera properly. He did love pop, though, and with it playing all day on the wireless, it's no wonder I followed him from an early age. I was given my first singles at age four—"Downtown" by Petula Clark and "Baby Love" by the Supremes, which I still have. Whilst Mum loved the crooners, specifically Frank Sinatra, Dad was a little rockier, preferring Frankie Laine and Connie Francis. He loved the Springfields and later the Seekers. I picked up the baton with Dusty (as well as Cilla and Sandie Shaw) and later the New Seekers. Next door, Geraldine loved the Everly Brothers and the Beatles. Jennifer proved a bit rockier still with the Rolling Stones and later, Jimmy Hendrix.

Mum taught me to read and write before I started school. And whatever the weather, she took me out shopping or to the park, the nearby Oakwood or Grovelands, for a walk and some air every day. Often Geraldine and Jennifer and the Tripp family dog, Kim, came too. Or Geraldine and her friend took me out. Shopping was generally at Eversley Parade, a short walk through Oakwood Park, or up at Southgate itself. I remember Timothy White's, the chemists, Williams Butchers, Murray and Brands, the toy shop, and I loved the old fridges with the clunk of their heavy doors at Express Dairies.

Mum also took me to the Southgate Odeon for family fare

such as *The Jungle Book*. We saw *Mary Poppins* when it came out but had to leave before the end, so Mum could get back to get the family tea ready for when Dad got home at six. I remember Dad taking me to see *Custer of the West* at one of the old cinemas in Enfield. With Auntie Doll, we three often went up to town to see a new release, *Chitty Chitty Bang Bang, The Great Waltz,* and *Scrooge* among them. Auntie Doll often took me on my own; we saw *Half a Sixpence* and memorably, *The Sound of Music*. I thought Julie Andrews was wonderful. Pantomime visits at Christmas included local productions at Golders Green. I remember being on the bus with Mum going to see *Cinderella* with Danny La Rue as an ugly sister. Mum always recalled being amazed that Danny La Rue was a man. I also remember seeing an old comedian, Tommy Trinder, in *Aladdin* there. We also saw glossier shows in town. We saw *Peter Pan* with Wendy Craig and, I think, Alastair Sim at the old Colosseum behind Tottenham Court Road one Christmas. Janet, her husband, Ben, and Susie and John came too. They arrived late, but I remember us all standing and waving from the front row as the cast took their bows. My favourite trip was in 1969, when we went to the London Palladium to see *Dick Wittington,* starring Tommy Steele and more specifically, Mary Hopkin, whom I loved at the time.

Once I went to primary school, St Andrews in Southgate, Mum went back to work. She dropped me off and picked me up each day. Her first job was at Tottenham Magistrates Court, something she loved. She took me once to visit, and I remember first standing in the courtroom and then going down narrow steps to the cells. I'm not sure why she left there. Maybe it was because longer term she couldn't have the school holidays off, which she wanted so that she could be back home to look after me. She moved to work in the early computer room at Southgate Technical College. She swore it was looking at screens all day in bad lighting that caused her to have to wear glasses later on.

My upbringing wasn't strict, but certain disciplines applied. I was certainly taught right from wrong. There were times when I was sent to my room which, with all my toys there, never seemed much of a punishment. And I was spanked on occasion, as we were at school in those days. Once as a teenager, I was making a puppet theatre, and Mum hit me with a light piece of wood with a nail in it. I had to go to hospital for a tetanus injection. Mum was mortified, of course, and told me to say my eyes were red, not from crying in pain, but from the heavy chlorine in a local swimming pool. I did, and I was never hit again. I was given a good moral foundation and have a solid set of values as a result. Mum and Dad were always the first to help others when they could. They listened to people's problems and tried to find solutions. Dad used to get very upset when he heard or read about children suffering or being treated badly.

I knew I was loved, well cared for, and looked after. A few years ago, I wrote a very short autobiography to help me understand my interests when I had to consider what I would like to do after being made redundant. I remember writing, 'As an only child, I wasn't spoilt with anything but love', and it was true. Mum, Dad, and I would do anything for one another. I hope I did for them as much as they did for me. Looking back, I wonder if I did.

My memories of childhood are very happy. I remember little things. Playing happily in my small box bedroom when not at school or out with friends, finding a sixpence from the tooth fairy under my pillow in place of the tooth I'd left there the night before, waiting at the front gate to spot Auntie Doll arrive when she came to visit, riding on the United Dairies' milk float with Bert the milkman, and riding my large three-wheeler bike round and round the garden.

Television, which I loved, was restricted to one hour a day on Mondays, Wednesdays, and Fridays. Shared family viewing was allowed at weekends. The BBC was preferred; ITV, apparently, was considered a bit common, but I do remember *Magpie* and series such as *Timeslip*. Restricted viewing, unfortunately, did mean I missed Thursday's *Blue Peter* with that great 1960s triumvirate Valerie Singleton, John Noakes, and Peter Purves, so I missed out on catchups at school the next day. However, I always got the *Blue Peter* annuals at Christmas.

For years we managed with an almost round-shaped black-and-white television. But in 1973, in time for Princess Anne's wedding to Captain Mark Phillips, we got our first colour set, rented from Rediffusion in Southgate. It was massive, housed in a wooden unit with sliding front doors, which I was most impressed with. When it was installed, tuned, and turned on, the first programme that appeared was *The Avengers* with Diana Rigg. We all loved that series, and Diana Rigg was set to feature quite significantly much later.

In later years, when Dad needed to sleep in the afternoons, Mum would watch old films on the television downstairs, recalling the many times she had gone to the cinema in her youth. She also loved the *Canal Journeys* series with Timothy West and Prunella Scales, and admired them both for their continued energy and zest for life. I had bought Mum the *Call the Midwife* books, and Mum and Dad thought the television series with Jenny Agutter was particularly realistic in reflecting the East End years of their youth. As a family, we all watched *Strictly Come Dancing*, although not together. Every Saturday, as soon as it ended, my phone would ring. 'So who's going this week?' Mum would ask, and we would talk about the performances the next day over lunch ahead of the Sunday results show. We were quite good at predicting who was to leave each week. How Auntie Doll would have loved that show had she still been around. She was a great dancer herself well into her eighties.

Mum and Dad both enjoyed reading. Dad liked political memoirs, football biographies, as well as more common, popular fiction such as books by Jeffrey Archer. As his eyesight started to diminish, he would listen to talking books which he and Mum selected from the library. One of Mum's favourite books, if not the favourite, was *Rebecca* by Daphne du Maurier, and she had the DVD of the film version which she watched many times. She had also enjoyed the television series with Diana Rigg as a very sinister Mrs Danvers. And there was also *The Shell Seekers* by Rosamunde Pilcher.

Dad wore glasses for as long as I can remember. In his youth he was a very handsome man. It was said he looked like the actor Alan Ladd, who apparently was also short. As well as being almost a year older than Dad, which was never mentioned for years. Mum was slightly taller, so she avoided wearing heels. I've inherited Dad's blonde hair, but he lost his early on, supposedly a result of overindulging in Brylcreem each day. He took care of himself and was vain to a degree, but in an amusing way; he was always able to laugh at himself when we ribbed him. Whenever we came back from a summer holiday, he wore a blue shirt on his first day back to work to accentuate his tan, and it did. He did his national service in the Royal Air Force, he said because it had the most flattering uniform, but later, with Jean and Norman (Jean had served in the Women's Royal Naval Service and at Bletchley Park during the war), Mum and Dad supported lots of Royal Air Force Association fundraising events, so his experience obviously generated a more lasting, noble sense of loyalty.

Dad loved the sun and always crossed to walk on the sunny side of the street, which matched his disposition. As a sportsman, he loved the outdoors, and whilst I didn't show any inclination for football or cricket, I was a good swimmer, taught solely by Dad in the sea and at Southgate, Arnos Grove, and Barrowell Green swimming pools.

In 1969, Mum and Dad sold 75 The Vale for £6,000 and followed the Tripps, who had moved a few years earlier, up the road to Winchmore Hill. Because 37 The Spinney was bigger, it felt as though we were moving up. I had a sizeable bedroom after the box room in The Vale. We also had a downstairs toilet.

Many happy years followed. I think Mum and Dad enjoyed being there more than in the previous house. Mum learned to drive and was a better driver than Dad, who tended to veer towards the middle of the road. He was also a terrible navigator. When he got lost, he wouldn't stop or turn back. He kept going until he got somewhere he thought he had heard of and then went from there. Mum used to get so annoyed. Geraldine has stories of his getting lost on the way back from holidays, taking hours to get home. She also remembers him reversing into a ditch in Solva once. Jean and their dog were in the back. The car, I think it was the Mini Traveller we had at the time, rammed up against the window as the car lay on its side. Norman and Richard had to tow the car out in the end. Geraldine and Jennifer thought it was very funny. Mum didn't, but we could all laugh about it in years to come. Of all the cars we had over the years—the Mini Traveller, the Austin 1100, the Austin Maxi, the Vauxhall Cavalier—Mum liked the rather sporty Ford Capri best. Mum would drive to work, and Dad commuted easily from the nearby Winchmore Hill British Rail Station, travelling in with Norman. I loved cycling to meet him in the evening when he came home. By the time I was around nine, I walked to school with children who lived across the road. After finishing at St Andrews Primary, I went to the fairly well-regarded Enfield Grammar School. I took the train for the first few years and then walked to save the fare.

I remember lots of good and fun times growing up in The Spinney. Once I got a pair of roller-skates, the old metal kind that slipped over normal shoes or plimsolls. Dad wanted a go and tried, falling flat on his back in the driveway in the process. Quite painful I think. He wasn't much good on my pogo stick or space hopper either.

Winchmore Hill was a safe and pleasant place to be, and good friends were made. There were always lots of neighbouring children about, and Groveland's Park was at the end of the road, very handy for walks and after-school play for me.

Shops and libraries weren't far away. When Mum was out shopping one day with Dad, he went off to collect the car, and Mum waited roadside for him to come back. To check, she asked a passing policeman, 'Is it all right to be picked up here?' to which he responded, 'Madam, at your age, I suggest you take any offer you get.' She was amused and told the story many times.

Mum loved the shops, as had Auntie Doll, who was a real West End girl at heart. Mum and Dad often visited me at Harrods when I worked there, enjoying my 40 per cent discount no doubt, and Mum and I frequently went to Oxford Street for clothes. Once I took Mum up to Jaeger in Regent Street with strict instructions from Dad to 'Make Mum get some things for herself.' She usually bought more for Dad and me on her trips. On this occasion, I waited outside whilst a very attentive assistant helped Mum try on loads of items. The thing that made the trip most enjoyable was the gentleman assistant's comment to Mum at some point, 'Would Madam like me to bring your husband inside to see what you have chosen?' Only a thirty-two-year age difference. Either Mum looked good, or I looked awful.

Once in The Spinney, Mum took up learning bridge. Jean already played, so Mum had a willing and handy partner. At first, Mum and Dad went to evening classes to learn the game. Dad did learn but wasn't particularly enthusiastic. He took up lawn bowls instead and played locally with Norman for years, taking care to polish and look after his woods. Whilst the bowls club provided quite a fun social life that Mum, Dad, Jean, and Norman could all get involved in, bridge needed competitive determination as well as pleasure, and Mum and Jean got good. Auntie Gertie had played for years already and at county level. As the older sister, it was clear that she didn't have much hope for Mum, but they soon ended up playing at the same clubs, and Mum and Jean did better. A few years later, Mum became a teacher herself, and whilst I despaired of the endless telephone analysis after each evening's bridge session, I was very proud of her, watching her prepare her student hand packs and writing instructional flip charts.

Bridge was something Mum certainly excelled in, and after years of not feeling particularly confident about her abilities, she was finally able to see how good she could be. But she was also an excellent home cook, as were Doll, Gertie, and Janet. Auntie Doll made the best roast potatoes, slicing lengthways rather than cutting in half, and I make them the same way. Much crispier. Veronica and Caroline are both very talented in the kitchen as well. When we went to visit, Veronica rarely served up less than five sweets, all of which she had to go through with Mum who insisted on the recipes. After he retired, Dad did his fair bit too. He made bread in terracotta plant pots, and his meatloaf was a favourite. It also became his job to prepare the vegetables for Sunday lunch. When we lived in The Vale, I remember our neighbours at one time cooking Mum and Dad their first curry, all hand prepared. I can picture them now, having to sit in the garden to eat it with numerous glasses of water to hand. They had never had anything like it or so hot before. Dad eventually became an expert in making his own curries.

Dad had always been an avid Tottenham Hotspur supporter, along with Norman and the rest of the Tripps, despite having been born nearer to West Ham. Mum followed football too; David Beckham could do no wrong. I always thought Mum supported Spurs too, and it was only much more recently that she revealed she preferred Arsenal. Her main interest was athletics, recalling her attendance at the 1948 London Olympic Games at White City and Wembley. Unfortunately, she wasn't able to attend the 2012 games but watched and followed daily.

Whilst we were at The Spinney, good holidays continued, and times seemed economically more stable for the most part. As well as holidaying with the Tripps in Wales and at Little Holland, we started to go further afield, to Devon and Cornwall, unless settling for the annual routine of going to Broadstairs. Dad's friend from the City, Ray Chatwin, had a property in St Peters, just on the outskirts of Broadstairs itself. At first, just the three of us went. But after a while, Ray, his wife, Joan, and their daughters, Dawn and Kim, joined us for the second week, all staying in the St Peters cottage. We had many happy times there. Dawn was three years older than me and Kim was three years younger, so Kim and I naturally bonded for days on the beach (Joss Bay), evening trips to Dreamland and the Lido in Margate, or visits to the cinema in Ramsgate to see the latest James Bond or whatever was on at the tiny Windsor in Broadstairs. Morelli's ice cream parlour in Broadstairs itself was also a favourite. We were soon joined by Dawn's boyfriend—now husband—Luke, but Dawn and Luke did their own thing most of the time under Ray's watchful eye. The first week away with just Mum and Dad was just as much fun, though—long days on the beach with picnics made with fresh rolls from the bakers next door to the cottage, evening walks along the cliffs, and when it rained, car rides up the coast through Sandwich to Deal, or the other way to Herne Bay. We saw Charles Hawtrey in a farce at the Dreamland Theatre; Lyn Paul, my New Seekers favourite, in summer season at the Margate Winter Gardens; and the three of us saw Jenny Agutter in *The Railway Children* at the Windsor cinema. It remained our all-time favourite film.

The Chatwins dabbled in antique dealing, running stalls at local specialist fairs and attending auctions, and we got into it too. Both Mum and Dad had a good eye and taste, and Mum started collecting Imari pottery in earnest. Dad liked the auctions. They built up a collection of nice, relatively good-quality pieces, and I amassed quite a number of things that I'm still very reluctant to part with.

As the seventies and eighties progressed, Mum and Dad were able to go abroad again, really for the first time since those cruises in the 1950s. With the Tripps they went to France, Spain, and Menorca, just the four of them at first. Later Jennifer, her husband, Gordon, their son George, and I often joined them, as did Gordon's mother, Janey, from Canada. When all together, we called the parental group the "Oldie Goldies". For them, breakfast was as much about their comparative medicine intake as it was about the food. Since they all tended to get up early each day, the rest of us had decided that when it got to around eleven in the morning, it was time to 'put them down' for a bit. Gordon would disappear into the kitchen and then emerge with jugs of his strong rum twizzlers, which they devoured. With the fresh air taking effect too, they were all out for the count for a few hours before the alfresco lunch arrived.

Mum had always loved holidays, but she had never felt the urge to travel that far. She had no desire to go to America, India, or the Far East, but she always said she wanted to go to Egypt. For some reason she seemed to have an affinity with the country, although her knowledge was only based on what she had read or seen on television. She mentioned it many times. Dad was content with fresh air, the sea, and sun, wherever that happened to be.

I remember the first thing Mum had to do when we arrived on holiday somewhere, book a hair appointment for later in the week. Although she didn't swim, merely paddled or stood in the sea, she said she would end up looking like *The Wreck of the Hesperus* if she didn't have an appointment. Mum had great hair, and she was very particular to take care of it. For years she went weekly to Channel Deux in Palmers Green and then, for over forty years, to Sue at the salon in Winchmore Hill. After Mum gave up driving and could no longer make it up the hill on foot without a struggle, she still went to see Sue, who kindly sent a taxi to collect her and drop her off. Mum was always well dressed and stylish, with a liking for scarves, upturned open-neck collars, bold necklaces, and brooches. But not hats. Quite ironic since Auntie Doll was a skilled and talented milliner, designing hats for the royal family on occasion. And after she retired, she took to dressmaking for herself, Mum, and others to great success.

For a number of years, I went skiing with my friends Mark and Jonathan, usually to Vermont in America, where we took advantage of the vast discounted shopping outlets on the drive up from Boston. I bought Dad and Mum loads of clothes there to bring back. Mum particularly liked the Kathryn Hepburn style of wide trousers I found her year on year from Van Heusen. We tried to get them back home but never found them. Mum certainly had her own signature style. She was never too trendy, but in the seventies, she wore maxi skirts and leather boots.

Whilst not overly religious, Mum and Dad were very Christian in their approach to others. And Dad liked the music of all the denominations he heard on *Songs of Praise*. Being of Welsh origin, whether from Abergavenny or elsewhere, we never found out, he thought he could sing. He couldn't really, but for a while he took to going to Sunday service at our local church, St Paul's, where I'd been christened, to sing and enjoy the hymns. At church ceremonies, christenings, weddings, or whatever, his voice could always be heard while the rest of us just mouthed the well-known verses. "Ave Maria" was a favourite.

Christmas was always an occasion to look forward to. We always had a real tree decorated with toys Dad and I had first starting buying each year from Woolworths in Southgate, and later with the baubles I bought from Harrods where I worked in the Christmas Decoration/ Garden Department in the year before I went off to college. In later years, we spent Christmas in The Spinney since it was harder for Mum, and especially Dad, to travel far, but always with Auntie Doll in tow. We mostly went to spend a few days with the Kirbys in

Berkshire or stayed in town and went to the Tripps's on Christmas Day before seeing the Chatwins on Boxing Day. At the Tripps's, we played loads of games, such as Bingo, Pit, and Newmarket. Geraldine remembers Mum saying, 'Don't count your winnings before the end of the game. It's bad luck.' Geraldine's daughters, Joanne and Vicky, and their families say it today. In Berkshire, lunch was originally at Uncle John and Auntie Winnie's above the shop in Crowthorne, which had now become a specialist off licence and sweet shop, having extended to new premises next door to carry on the grocery business. Cousin John and Veronica were there of course; Stephen and Lorraine had moved to Hull, where Stephen became a prominent professor in politics. Winnie cooked at first, but when poor Uncle John started to get unwell, and Winnie started relying on the sherry a bit too much (easily accessible from the downstairs shop), Veronica took over, and indeed did most of the caring for Uncle John in his final years as well as work long hours all day in the grocery shop. Once John and Winnie had gone, we naturally went to John and Veronica's.

When I was small, I had a pillowcase rather than a stocking to wake up to on Christmas morning. It was full of goodies and topped up with fruit.

We didn't see so much of Dad's family, certainly not at Christmas, although we visited his mum, my nana, and sister, Norma, and her husband, Charlie, who all still lived in Homerton. Brothers Reg and Don lived with Nana, so we saw them too. Norma and Charlie lived nearby, off Morning Lane, with their children, Denise and Colin, both older than me. Sister Joan had moved to run a hotel with her husband, Vic, in Gloucestershire, and we went there a number of times. Dad wrote to Joan until she died. He also kept in contact with Denise, who moved to St Albans after she married David. Mum was very fond of Reg, Norma, and Charlie. Don was my other godfather, but Mum and Dad used to say it should have been Reg.

Mum loved decorating the Christmas tree and looking again at the collection of things we'd collected over the years, some getting increasingly tatty. We never threw them out until they were completely broken. An angel, for many years the one from Woolworths, or a star topped the tree, and we had a robin and china dove pinned onto the bottom branches. Mum loved watching and feeding the birds in the garden, particularly the robins which came every day. 'Feed the birds and you will never want,' Grandma Edie always said. Cousin John and Gertie hated birds and rarely had the windows open in case they flew in.

In 1978 I left school. I had done quite well except in Latin O-level, although Mum and Dad had needed to pay for me to have extra French lessons, which I hated, and tutoring in maths from Dawn Chatwin's boyfriend, Luke. I gained a place at the University College of North Wales, Bangor, but I deferred taking it for a year, working instead at Enfield Library, where I'd had a Saturday job, and then as a shop assistant at Harrods, where I was to return whilst I waited for a "proper job" after graduating. I remember Mum saying to me once, 'Never work in Harrods, in the theatre or for the BBC.' Not only did I end up working at Harrods for thirteen years after college—the "proper" job never came, and I enjoyed it and progressed well—I switched from studying economics after my first year at Bangor to do drama. In recent years, I have helped support human resource consulting projects for the BBC.

Dad drove me off to college, a five and a half-hour car journey in those days, and admitted feeling very sad leaving me there so far away from home. I know Mum missed me too, and I was homesick on occasion, once I remember when playing Monopoly with all the London streets. But Mum and Dad visited often despite the long drive, and I came home on the odd occasion. Dad used to write to me weekly, and now and again send me bars of chocolate from Thorntons. Mum, Dad, and Auntie Doll came up for my graduation and saw me in *Fiddler on the Roof* at Theatre Gywnedd. I had chosen to stay on in Bangor for the summer season productions, alternating *Fiddler* with a part in *Chicago*, a role in which I was 'delightfully amusing' according to the *Liverpool Echo*. Interestingly, Mum and Dad didn't comment on my performance, although they liked the show, and I think they were relieved when I came home and started working properly, even if it was back in Harrods. Years later, the three of us saw a production of *Fiddler* at the Victoria Apollo in London.

After returning from college, I lived at home for a few years before buying my first flat in Palmers Green. I got a mortgage of three times my salary, and to make up the £32,000 purchase price along with my saved deposit, Mum and Dad guaranteed £7,000, for which I was very grateful. It was at this time I got into the habit of going home every Sunday for lunch, something I have done ever since, although Mum and Dad have never protested if I had something else to do with friends. More lately though, they did ask to see me on the Saturday if I was busy on the Sunday. At first I took home my washing for Mum to do; I didn't have room for a machine of my own. Naturally the roles later reversed, and I shopped and did chores for them as they found things more difficult. It was the least I could do.

Mum and Dad helped with getting the flat in order, buying me things and helping with decorating. When I moved later to Islington, buying Jennifer's garden flat on her marriage to Gordon, they came over regularly, again helping to decorate. No one cleaned windows as well as my father, and he often blackened the chimney grate for me with Zebo polish or buffed up the brass fender. Dad and my friend John once put up a whole line of trellis along a garden wall to give me extra security while I was busy working. More important, Mum and Dad enjoyed helping me tend the garden, and as with their own at The Spinney, they created a nice garden for me. The only thing they were slightly unhappy with was the fact I was in Islington, that is, close to the East End. which they still regarded as relatively down on its heels. Things had changed considerably since they moved out, but it took a while for them to see it. The same feelings resurfaced when Nolan and I bought the apartment at Hackney Wick. They did see it during construction, when I drove them over one Sunday. Seeing the Olympic Park and Stadium gave them some relief, and triggered memories for Dad of rowing on the River Lee and canal there. And the proximity to Hackney Marshes brought back lots of stories from Mum.

In 1996 we celebrated Mum and Dad's fortieth wedding anniversary. This was the first big party they had held I think. Maybe money wasn't so much of an issue, and it was a milestone anniversary after all. We had a meal at West Lodge near Cockfosters. Close family came—Cousin John, Veronica, Angela, Caroline, and Gordon—along with the Tripps of course and a few selected friends. I had a special cake made by a friend of mine, Matheus, the head patisserie chef at Harrods, with a hand of cards on it for Mum and bowling woods for Dad.

After I had moved out, I tried to go over as much as I could in addition to the Sunday visits. We enjoyed going out for lunch and into town when we could. My friend Mark worked at the Peoples

Palace restaurant at the Royal Festival Hall for a number of years, and I took Mum and Dad there to watch the boat procession on the Thames to mark the fiftieth anniversary of D-Day, which they found very moving. Mark joined us for dinner afterwards, so we had a riverside seat to continue to watch the old boats pass by. In later years, though, Dad got tired easily as by then he was suffering from numerous things, such as angina, high blood pressure, mini strokes, increasing deafness, and failing eyesight. So trips further afield weren't as frequent. However, he was nosy and very sociable, so he still tried to get out as much as he could. When he couldn't make it, Mum still did, although trips to the West End, Enfield, and Hatfield to John Lewis or even to the local nurseries became less frequent. Obviously their summer fruit-picking trips in Hertfordshire had stopped years before, but Mum did seem to manage to go with Jean daily to Sainsbury's at Winchmore Hill. Jenifer, Geraldine, Dad, Norman, and I could never quite understand the fascination; nothing much seemed to be purchased. But I took Mum once, and it took her over an hour to get round. She knew so many people there to chat to, customers and staff alike. And then with a coffee at the in-house Starbucks factored in, we realised it was a way for them to keep in touch with people and simply socialise when other options were disappearing.

There had always been a good restaurant on the Green at Winchmore, on the site of the old King Easton garden nursery. For the last few years it's been Buckle and Vaughan. Mum and Dad celebrated their fiftieth wedding anniversary there with friends, including the full Tripp clan. Whenever Mum went there, often just the two of us when we went to visit Dad during his many hospital stays, she recounted the story of Jean buying a large print of a winter landscape by Bruegel from the King Easton nursery, and she told the story to the waiters again that night. The print took pride of place above Jean and Norman's fireplace. Mum and Dad had it above theirs when Jean moved into care. I have it now.

Caroline and I had also arranged a private room at Rules in Covent Garden for a family celebration, combining Mum and Dad's fiftieth with John and Veronica's fortieth. Stephen and Lorraine, now living in France, came over, bringing their son Matthew. I had been a pageboy for Stephen and Lorraine at their wedding when I was four, paired up with Janet's daughter Susie as bridesmaid. The two of us repeated the roles two years later at John and Veronica's wedding. For the anniversary lunch, I arranged for a massive chocolate opera cake to finish off the meal. By this time, 2006, having been so much younger than her now-departed siblings, Mum had become the matriarch of the Kirby family, a role she loved. Family came first, and although she wasn't again able to see everyone as often as she would have liked, she talked to John and Veronica often, as well as to Stephen and Lorraine.

Mum and I did make it to Essex once, though, to a family gathering Cousin Stephen put together after years of doing family research. Mum saw her very elderly uncle Stanley, who I had never heard of before, and the place was packed with those of us who knew each other alongside various distant cousins, twice, three, or four times removed. I remember thinking as an only child how strange it was to be related to so many people.

I see Caroline whenever she is in London, so I have always been able to keep Mum updated as to how the younger generation has been doing, particularly Angela and Stephen's son Matthew, who I keep in contact with when we can. We didn't know that we were to lose Cousin John so soon after the family celebration. Mum was devastated, but I can remember how well she dealt with it, balancing emotions and grief alongside practicalities. Dad wasn't well enough to come, but I took Mum to Oxfordshire to see John in his final weeks, which gave her the chance to see him for what she knew would be one last time and help her prepare for the inevitable end. Dad wanted so much to see John again. The two got on well.

Mum and I went down again for the cremation and the wonderful celebratory memorial church service, to which so many people came and where Caroline spoke. And we listened to "Bring Me Sunshine" by Morecambe and Wise. Of course, all surviving family members were there, including Cousin Janet, who we hadn't seen, or indeed heard of for years. Janet herself died not long after.

Buckle and Vaughan hosted a small lunch we had for Mum's ninetieth birthday in 1998. Mum didn't want to do anything at first, probably because Dad, by this time, was bedridden at home and so unable to join. But along with a tremendous party session at Sue the hairdressers the day before, she appreciated and enjoyed the fuss made. Geraldine and Richard, and Jennifer and Gordon came along to represent our old and constant friends and second family, the Tripps.

We had always enjoyed going out to eat when it could be afforded. A treat when I was very young was going with Mum and Dad to the Italian restaurant in Winchmore Hill, near the old Green Dragon pub. They did wonderful ice cream profiteroles, and we always brought Mum and Dad's empty Mateus Rose wine bottle home to stick a candle in. At the time, as we began to move away from the traditional British meat-and-two-veg staples, it all seemed very exotic.

When Mum worked at Southgate Technical College, she often

took us to eat at the small restaurant there, where we could sample the food cooked by the catering students. Mum also took me once to see Cliff Richard at the college. He was there giving a spiritual talk to students, so he didn't sing, but we both liked him. I had a Cliff picture on my wall for a time. I remember it was removed when I was naughty, along with my—preferred—Lyn Paul and New Seekers posters.

As Mum and Dad progressed and had entered their late eighties, they were still comfortable in The Spinney, although age was naturally taking its toll. They often said they should have moved somewhere smaller when they had more energy. Mum would have liked a country cottage, probably near Cousin John and Veronica, but they were conscious of their friends and support network in London, and I think that's what held them back.

By his eighties, Dad was in and out of hospital quite regularly with a number of infections or complaints, as well as more serious scares such as angina and mini strokes. He ultimately became bedbound, relying on Mum who selflessly and, mainly without complaint, cooked, cleaned, and generally cared for him. He was a good patient. Mum and Dad did have the support of a non-medical carer, who Dad was fond of, and she did her best I'm sure, despite bringing three young children with her each time she came, which didn't help. It was Mum, though, who was there full time, which obviously did wear her down. Dad saw this; regretfully, I preferred not to. However, Mum herself seemed strong and relatively fit, if tired, and remained positive and still looked to the future, wanting to make sure I was going to be all right. She did have her swollen ankles, and she suffered from painful arthritis and rheumatism as time went on. She was devastated that walking was becoming more uncomfortable. 'I never thought I'd be unable to walk,' she said.

I was able to go over and see them at least once a week, so I did what I could to help. There were times I know when I didn't seem particularly sympathetic because, selfishly, I didn't like to see them decline. There was a degree of denial on my part. I wanted them to be who they always had been. Mentally, both had their full faculties, but physically, Dad was becoming a virtual invalid, and Mum was becoming increasingly shattered, terrified she would wake up one day and find Dad lifeless. She was already in the habit of waking up in the night to check his breathing.

Despite the onset of age and its associated problems, both were determined to stay together in the house. At times they did think that care homes might have to be an option in the future. They saw how settled Jean had become after she moved to one, but for as long as possible, 37 The Spinney was going to remain their home. They wanted it to be my inheritance, and with friends and neighbours nearby, such as Katie, Fionulla, and Andy and their children, and with Jean not far away, The Spinney was where they were determined to stay. And so we carried on as best we could. I think Mum and Dad were happy. I hope so.

# Chapter 2

## MUM

In February last year, things started happening that changed life forever. I had been working in the West End for a small HR consulting business, a minor position compared to my past managerial roles, but one which I hoped would keep me going for a few years, until I retired. During the week, I would speak to, and on occasion argue with, Mum about four times a day, starting with the first call, just after eight o'clock, before I went into the office. One day, our early morning call had been pretty standard as usual, brief as we had no news since speaking the night before, but they had both had a good night and were about to have breakfast before the carer arrived to get Dad ready for the day. A little later though, Mum called. Dad had been taken ill again, which wasn't uncommon, but on the carer's advice, an ambulance had been called. Being bedbound, Dad was frail, although strong at heart, but he had been prone to catching infections, mainly caused by the infrequent visits from the district nurse to change his catheter. With his history of mini strokes, angina, poor blood pressure, blood disorder, and general inability to move much, Mum watched him constantly and worried about him rather than about herself. Whilst he had been in and out of hospital many times in the past, sometimes with major scares, he had always fought back and returned to some degree of normality. This time, though, he wasn't eating or drinking, which was odd. He was shaking and appeared to be slightly delirious. Mum asked if I could come home, which of course I did. My bosses and colleagues were aware of my parents' situation and were always understanding and sympathetic. I arrived just in time for the ambulance. Dad was not good this time, and Mum was extremely distressed, so much so that the ambulance men suggested I stay to watch her rather than go with Dad, which I did. As Dad was taken away, Mum collapsed onto the hall chair and said tearfully that she was convinced this was the end for Dad. She kept saying, 'I did what I can. I've tried as best as I could.' It was heartbreaking to see Mum like this. I could only reassure her that she couldn't have done more, that she had been wonderful, and how Dad was so appreciative of her taking care of him. I said Dad had fought back before and no doubt would do again.

It was at this time that I began to worry that I hadn't done enough for either of them. Yes, I saw them at least once a week, spoke daily, and took Mum out shopping locally or to see friends such as Jean at her care home. I helped clean, cooked, bought them things, decorated, did odd jobs in the house and garden, helped manage the finances and household matters, put the bins out and all of that, but could I have done more? And what could I do now? I still had to work. I lived away and had my independence. Later, Mum said the last thing she and Dad wanted was for me to lose that independence or stop leading a life of my own, in the same way that Herbert, her dad, and Edie had insisted Mum had to carry on when they were in poor and declining health.

I stayed with Mum for a while and settled her in bed. Then I went to the hospital, the local North Middlesex, which they both hated, Mum in particular. 'You never come out of there alive', she said, a sentiment echoed by the Tripps, who had seen Norman catch one infection after another there in his final weeks not long before. When I got there, it seemed that Dad had been taken care of quickly, luckily. Injections, wires as before. He was seemingly stable when I got to him, although exhausted and still pretty much out of it, so he didn't know I was with him. Apparently he wasn't in danger, but rightly, they needed to observe him. He was moved to a ward for the night at least, they said.

I went home to Mum's and stayed the night, to make sure she ate, slept, and took her blood pressure medication. The next morning I left early and caught the first train to the office. I let myself in to collect my laptop and divert the main office line to my mobile so that I could work remotely. I left a message and then returned to be with Mum, who was a little calmer, before going to see Dad.

Dad stayed in hospital for three days, and again, pulled through, as he had done in the past. I had stayed with Mum throughout, working from home and going back and forth to the hospital. When Dad was brought home, he wept. He had thought he would never see Mum or home again.

With continued support from Mum, neighbours, district nurses, and the carer, Dad seemed to get his strength back, as much as it was. I returned to Hackney Wick and the office, and we all carried on again.

Not long after this scare, days later I think, with Dad back at home, Mum herself sounded rather odd when I called her on my first morning call. Different from how she had been the evening before. She knew where she was, had made the tea as usual, but was saying that she was 'seeing things'. She said someone was sitting on the bed next to her, and when she looked out the front window, she said she could see two people sitting in her car. People were also digging up the pavement and planting trees, and the skaters in the Bruegel picture downstairs appeared to be moving. And a song was constantly playing in her head. She wasn't frightened and knew she had to be imagining things, but she wasn't sure why this was happening. Despite the tiredness, Mum had always been strong and healthy, taking only a few blood pressure tablets a day, which was good for someone at the age of near ninety-one. She was getting a bit forgetful and worried that she wasn't as astute with money matters as she had been, which she knew was down to age, but otherwise she just felt tired, if not exhausted at times. She passed the phone to Dad, and he said that Mum wasn't panicking, or acting strangely, but things weren't quite right. All three of us agreed to see what the carer thought when she arrived. I told Mum I would call back in a bit.

I called again within half an hour, hoping the carer had arrived on time. She had, and whilst not medically qualified, her view was that Mum might have an infection which was causing the hallucinations. We called the doctor, who seemed to think our diagnosis might be right. He promised to visit as quickly as he could. My parents had a long and positive association with their local surgery and were fortunate to benefit from home visits by a doctor on the occasions an emergency arose, particularly since Dad couldn't be moved. It appeared that Mum was still thinking with some rationality and was aware of what was happening, so I stayed in the office until we got a better idea of the situation.

It took a few hours for the doctor to get to the house, but fortunately Mum was still functioning and bearing up well whilst we waited. He confirmed Mum had a urinary infection, a common complaint in the elderly, often brought on by dehydration. Mum always made sure Dad drank lots of water, but she stuck to constant cups of tea, although she never finished them. Mum was dehydrated. The doctor prescribed a three-day course of tablets to be taken regularly throughout the day, starting immediately. I spoke to her, and she assured me she had started taking them, and whilst the visions persisted, they certainly hadn't gotten any worse. As the three days progressed, and the course of tablets took effect, things improved; the visions seemed to go away. Mum was actually amused by it all but did feel another course of medication might be sensible, just to make sure the infection had completely cleared up. The doctor told her that, unfortunately, without hospital admission, he could only prescribe the one three-day course. So she took nothing more.

With Mum promising to drink more water as well as her tea, we hoped that would be the end of it. Through her many subsequent phone calls to friends, Mum learnt that a lot of other people she knew had similar infections over the years and been able to keep it at bay, so no one was unduly concerned. And she knew what she had to do—drink more.

Dad turned ninety on 14 February, Saint Valentine's Day. He had always joked he was certain to get cards on the day, although all were for the birthday. We celebrated as best we could. I had the day off, and we had sandwiches and cake by his bedside accompanied by red wine. He certainly received his usual fair share of cards and presents of shirts and sweets. As he got older, he didn't ask for much. We had a nice time.

As I was going to be elsewhere on Sunday, I went over to Mum and Dad's as planned early in the morning of the Saturday on the last weekend in February. When I arrived, the carer's mother, deputising that day and an ex-carer herself, was outside. She couldn't get in, and no one was answering either the door or the phone. The carer had front door keys, but Mum used to bolt the main door from the inside every night before going to bed. Then she unlocked it when she went downstairs to make the tea in the morning. The door still seemed to be bolted on the inside. Not wanting to panic—it was still quite early, so perhaps Mum and Dad were sleeping—I tried my keys, knocked, shouted up, and called both the house phone and the mobile. No response. I went down the drive to the back of the house and tried calling up from there. Again no response. I then started getting worried; surely either Mum or Dad would have heard something even if they had been sleeping. The back gate was locked, so I moved the rubbish bins to the fence and managed to climb over so I could bang loudly on the back windows. Still no response. I'd unlocked the gate for the carer, and we were joined by a neighbour who had heard the noise and had come to see how they might help. I can't remember what was going through my mind, but I knew I had to get in somehow. I broke the kitchen window using an old brick from the garden. As I was unpicking the glass from the frame, calling out, Mum tentatively crept down the stairs, very disorientated. Asking if she was all right didn't get a response. She was dishevelled; she had her pyjamas on, but no dressing gown. I went to check on Dad whilst the carer went to Mum. He seemed to be comfortable, as much as he ever was by now, but was very distressed. He had woken up to hear Mum wandering around looking for certain cards, talking to herself, or then asking Dad for particular clubs or diamonds, and so on. She wasn't making any sense and wasn't talking rationally. Back upstairs with the carer by now, this behaviour was continuing. Dad was shouting desperately at Mum to try and get her to calm down, answer him, or explain what was happening. He was otherwise helpless, lying there in bed with failing eyesight and hearing. It must have been so frightening for him. We did our best to pacify Dad whilst Mum continued to ramble, panicking now that she needed 'the trick' to avoid 'losing the house'. Mum then started shouting, obviously in desperation as in her mind, we weren't helping or giving her the cards she wanted. I got her back on the bed. Very calmly she looked at me and said, 'Can I just ask you one thing?' I said yes. She said, 'Just give me the twelve of diamonds. I just need that to get the trick.'

Then it struck me; it was bridge language.

I said I didn't have the card. She then said I was useless and didn't or couldn't understand. The same thing with Dad when he again tried to reason and get her to talk sense. The situation was horrendous. Mum had never been like this before, and as her anger developed, the things she said to Dad and I became vindictive and accusatory. I know none of it was meant, but she was lashing out, focused on these ridiculous cards and the game her mind was playing.

Dad was excellent despite his concern. Worried and frustrated, of course, but fully aware we needed to call the doctor, which we did. We were told it would be a while before anyone could come out; it was a Saturday. Before the carer left, we fed and settled Dad, and I called a glazier to come and fix the broken window.

We three then stayed together in their shared bedroom. I gave them drinks. Mum did drink some tea, but she remained fixated on the cards. She spoke of nothing else. She obviously knew we were with her, as she referred to us by name when demanding cards. But she couldn't be calmed or pacified. I tried to dress her, but she fought to get up, to go in search of a certain card. Dad started becoming agitated again, naturally, as he was so frustrated at not being able to help. But he couldn't even get up to hold her. 'Please stop talking about those bloody cards,' he repeatedly said.

Whilst waiting for the doctor, the glazier came and fixed the window, demanding £850 in cash by ten o'clock that night. If I didn't have the cash when he came back to collect it, he said he would take the window out and take it back. This obviously couldn't be right; the glazier was recommended on the internet. But I didn't have time to fight or report him. In the end, the neighbours very kindly loaned me the money so I could pay that night.

The doctor arrived mid-afternoon. He examined Mum, who was actually quite calm at first. She knew a doctor was there as she kept saying 'I'm not sick. There's nothing wrong with me.' I remember thinking, *Oh, why doesn't she mention the cards?* Most of what we had described to the doctor seemed to have stopped, and I wanted him to see what Mum had been like so he could work out what was wrong, as something clearly was.

Card talk soon resumed though, so he did see. He said Mum had a temperature, palpitations, high blood pressure, and he suspected the infection had returned. Mum would need to go into hospital, the North Middlesex, for treatment and observation. At this, Mum screamed, 'I'm not going in there. You die in there. You never get out!' She started crying. I held her hand and tried to reassure her that it wouldn't be for long, and it was for the best. Dad, upset himself, said the same. She kept repeating, 'I'm not ill.' The doctor called for the ambulance and left, and the three of us waited.

I called the carer. Dad could not be left alone if I had to go to the hospital with Mum. She agreed to come over when the ambulance arrived; she wasn't that far away. Mum was a bit quieter while we waited, probably having exhausted herself. She hadn't wanted to eat and had drunk little. I could only tell her, over and over, that it would be all right, and she would get the care she needed for the infection once and for all.

The ambulance arrived quite quickly although Mum wasn't considered an emergency. As it arrived, so did the glazier demanding his money. The carer wasn't there yet, so I was going to have to wait with Dad until she arrived before I could go to the hospital.

Before the paramedics helped guide Mum downstairs from the bedroom to the ambulance, she went over to Dad's bed, leaned over, kissed him on the head, and said, 'I love you.' Dad said, 'And I love you too. See you very soon.'

The ambulance then took Mum away.

It wasn't too long before I was able to leave Dad and get to the hospital, to Mum. The paramedics had told me where she was being taken, not emergency, but to an admissions ward. Dad understood I might be gone some time, but I would be back to stay with him overnight and until Mum came home. We both thought Mum was likely to be in hospital for a few days, until the infection had started to clear up and a longer course of tablets prescribed.

I found where Mum had been taken. The ward was busy and full. I'm not sure what type of ward it was, but it seemed like a sort of holding area. Mum had been allocated a bay with bed and chair, but I found her wandering around, asking anyone for cards and calling out for help as she needed to 'get the trick'. She was still in her pyjamas, dressing gown, slippers, and cardigan, now hanging loosely off her. She did not look good, and I wondered whether she was warm enough.

She was agitated and disorientated, but when she realised who

I was said, 'Listen to me, I know you don't understand, but you must have a diamond', or spade, or whatever it was. When I said I didn't and asked how I could get it, she got increasingly agitated. We could not talk properly. Again she kept saying, 'I'm not ill', and asking, 'What am I doing here?' She could not take in anything I was saying back to her. I managed to get her to sit in the chair, still talking to herself, me, or to anyone in neighbouring beds about cards, tricks, the game, and such like. Not wanting to leave her in case she wandered again, but needing to find someone to talk to, I asked one of the staff whom I could speak to. The response was the usual, 'Someone will be along to talk to you as soon as they can.' I sat with Mum and waited. I called Dad to tell him I was with Mum, and we were waiting to find out what was going to happen. I said I would be home soon. He was slightly reassured that I was there and that Mum wasn't alone, but he was obviously concerned. I was worried for him as well as for Mum.

Someone did come along to speak to me shortly afterwards. I don't know whether they were a doctor or nurse. They said someone would come to sit with Mum to monitor her, but she would need to be kept in overnight for observation, followed by tests in the morning. That wasn't any surprise. I explained what medication she took for her blood pressure, which local GP she was with, what the situation was at home, her no doubt being exhausted from looking after Dad, her general health history, when she had had the previous infection, and what had been happening in the hours before she was admitted. They said they were going to try and get her to drink and would probably have to give her a mild sedative to help her rest.

I felt helpless but did get her onto the bed at least. Someone came with another chair, sat with her, and told me she would not be left alone. I'm not sure how long I stayed, I but decided I could leave her and get back to Dad to relieve the carer.

When I got home, I told Dad what seemed to be happening and that I would stay over and then go back to the hospital in the morning. I decided that although the carer would be visiting Dad at certain times throughout the day, I wanted to be there. I wanted to cook his meals, get him to drink, and keep him company when he wasn't sleeping, which he now did a lot, night and day. Dad was pleased to hear I would be with him.

We both got through the night relatively well. I slept in Mum's bed next to Dad's.

The next morning, once the carer arrived, I drove home to collect a few things, including my work laptop, on the assumption I might have to be with Dad for a few days and would need a change of clothes and be able to work from home. I explained what was happening to Nolan. He was well-aware of my dad being an invalid and needing increasing trips to hospital, but he was quite shocked that this time the problem was with Mum. I also called a few members of the family and some of Mum and Dad's close friends to let them know about Mum and how Dad and I were managing the situation.

I think it was while I was still at the flat that the hospital called. I had given my mobile number as the contact rather than Mum and Dad's home line. Whoever it was told me not to worry, but Mum had fallen in the night and knocked her head. They said they had scanned her, and there did not appear to be any injury or damage but that there would inevitably be bruising. They said it was likely she had fallen because the sedatives had made her woozy and unsteady on her feet. I said I was on the way there and felt relieved that they had said she was all right. I didn't ask about how she was generally as I just wanted to get there.

When I arrived, Mum had been moved to room of her own. She looked dreadful, tired, grubby, with plasters on her head and on her elbow. I was struck how thin her arms were. She was on the bed. A nurse or support assistant was sitting with her. She recognised me but still wasn't talking sense. I kissed her and said I loved her, something I realised I should have done more often. She said she loved me too. *That seems to be something,* I thought. *Some degree of normality.* I asked the assistant if I could talk to someone, and she went to fetch the consultant or doctor in charge. While I waited, I tried to talk about normal things—that Dad sent his love, missed her, but was all right. That I was staying with him until she came home. How I had seen the birds in the garden that morning, looking to nest. Nothing much seemed to register. Unfortunately, Mum had been given a jumbo-sized pack of playing cards, probably with good intentions, but they just served to focus her even more on her preoccupation, if not obsession, with her need to complete the trick. In fact, it probably made things worse. Now with some actual cards available, Mum seemed to be trying to sort them into hands as she used to do when preparing and teaching. Whatever she was trying to do, though, only seemed to make her more anxious.

A doctor came in to see me. Being a Sunday, they would not start tests properly until the next day, but they were able to confirm that Mum did indeed have another infection for which they had prescribed tablets. However, they had been trying to get her to take them, along with those for her blood pressure. I could see a dose of tablets in the little plastic tub left on her table. They said she had not been drinking much either, but they hoped to get her to eat and drink something as she settled. I asked what I could do. There was nothing other than tell her how important the medication was, and try and get her to drink and take the tablets. I seem to remember I had some success and asked if we could try tea rather than the water or juice which was also on the table. When the tea came, a little was drunk. Other than that, we just had to wait to see how things developed. I asked how long it might take, and they couldn't say.

After a while, when I had helped Mum to the toilet, she was able to say she wanted to go and was able to walk there with support. I managed to get her to lie down on the bed, the cards still in her hands. I kissed her again, told her to sleep, and said I was going to get Dad his lunch and would be back the next day. I repeated that she must take her tablets for me and for Dad, and told her to get them to call me if she needed anything. I don't think much of what I said was taken in, but Mum seemed a little calmer. I was reassured that someone was to be with her in the room constantly, day and night.

I went home to Dad. The carer had left by then. I cooked lunch, having stocked up at the supermarket on the way back. Dad's first thoughts, and questions were of Mum. What could I say? The person I had left in the hospital bed was not my mother, but I couldn't tell Dad that. I needed to look after him. I told him most of the truth. Mum was in a nice room whilst they monitored her. She was being given medication for the new infection, and tests would follow the next day. She had fallen over and banged her head slightly, but she had been checked over, and she was all right. She seemed tired, was talking, but needed to sleep. 'Has she stopped going on about the cards?' he asked. 'No' I said, 'it will take a while for the tablets to kick in.'

In a way, the rest of Sunday followed our usual pattern. Dad slept a bit, we had cups of tea, I put the bins out, we had a bit of supper, and the carer returned to change him and put him down for the night, which always tended to be around nine o'clock. We said we loved one another, a habit we had gotten into each evening, dating from one of the occasions he had been in hospital. Despite failing eyesight, Dad was still capable of using a simple, large button mobile phone, and we used to talk to say goodnight wherever he was. He always spoke to Mum, too, when he was away. Despite poor hearing, he was able to hear pretty well if the volume was turned up to its highest.

I wanted to look after Dad so much. I remembered a few years earlier, when Dad had again been in hospital, this time in Barnet. One day it had been snowing heavily, and I wasn't able to drive over to see him at the hospital as promised. I was upset, but Mum said Dad would understand I couldn't get there and knew that I would do anything to look after him if I could. Now I hoped that Mum, somewhere in her mind, knew I would do the same for her too.

I watched a bit of television that night and then went upstairs to sleep. We heard nothing more from the hospital, and I think we both had a relatively good night.

Mum stayed in that hospital room for the next two weeks. I now struggle to remember exactly what happened day by day or in what order, but Dad and I seemed to fall into a pattern to deal with the situation, waiting and hoping for things to quickly return to normal and we could get Mum home again, safe and well. Over that period, I stayed in The Spinney with Dad and worked from there. My bosses were very supportive, although the volume of work didn't let up.

I continued to sleep in Mum's bed, next to Dad's. He had little awareness of time and frequently woke up in the night. At first, I would get up and make him a cup of tea, but after a few days, I just told him to go back to sleep for a bit. He liked me nagging; it reminded him of Mum. In the mornings we had tea and waited for the carer to arrive to clean Dad, dress him, and give him breakfast. The carer came at least twice a day, more if we needed it and she could manage it. In those two weeks, I would call the hospital early, but there was generally nothing they could tell me over the phone. I went to see Mum each morning, taking clean clothes and other essentials. Mum seemed to be calmer overall when I was with her. Her head and arms were clearing up, although her arm was still bruised and tender. There were days when I couldn't get any sense from her at all; the cards featured continually. She had also started to say that the doctors were trying to kill her. She wanted me to get the police. She believed she had been kidnapped during the night and taken to the basement. She thought she had lost the house. I found those times hard to deal with. Stupidly, when I think of it now, I had taken Mum's mobile in for her to call me if she needed anything. This resulted in her calling me, Geraldine, Jennifer, and others day and night, pushing any button she could from her saved contacts. Always in a state of panic, calling for the police to come as she felt in danger. Once when I arrived, she broke down completely. 'They told me you were dead,' she said. I could only hold her and tell her I wasn't going anywhere.

At times we were able to have a degree of normal conversation. I updated her on Dad, Jean, Katie, and others. I showed her photographs of the garden, particularly the blossoming camellia which she loved. She told me she wanted to get home, needed to get her hair done, and find a way to take Dad away to the sea again. Mum spoke about the different assistants who had been sitting with her. Some she liked, others she didn't. One had told her how beautiful she was. 'I've never been called beautiful in my life!' she said. He was her favourite, despite having, 'robbed me of the house and kidnapping me last night.' She told me she had invited some of them home for steak and champagne once she got back. Somehow, in amongst all the incomprehension, we managed to laugh at things now and again. When I told her I loved her or kissed her, she asked, 'What are you being so soppy for?'

I massaged her feet with Nivea; she said it smelled lovely. Amazingly, for the first time in about thirty years, the swelling on her ankles disappeared. 'My ankles are back,' she said and laughed. She could sometimes make sense of the television, recognising programmes and locations, although more often than not, the cards she wanted were in the television somehow, and she had to get them. One morning I found her in a different room, sitting at a table reading newspapers. We went through them, talking about politics, Andy Murray's latest health problems, and Tottenham Hotspur and football transfers. *This is surely a glimmer of hope,* I thought, but it wasn't to last.

Friends were kind enough to visit her—Jennifer, Fionulla, who with her husband Andy and their family had always been such good neighbours, and Sue from the hairdressers. The carer and her mother also took time to go in, although Mum did not recognise her children who went in too.

I spoke to a number of doctors, consultants, and specialists. There seemed so many of them, always different. There were signs that the infection was clearing up, but Mum was still not taking her tablets regularly, which I knew, or, it seemed her blood pressure medication. Thinking they were part of the conspiracy to kill her, she refused. They tried hiding tablets in her food, but without me there to feed her, she wouldn't eat the food for similar reasons—it was poisoned. I had been able to get back to my flat to get a few things once or twice, and I brought back some olive oil cake Nolan had made, which she ate and loved. Any other food I took in—fruit, sandwiches, chocolate, and biscuits—she would eat. And she would drink any tea, water, or juice I got for her. I told her the food they were providing was food I had brought in, to try and get her to eat when I wasn't there. Similarly, I told her that the medicine she was being given and needed to take was sent through me by her own doctor, so it was safe to have. But unless I was there, she rarely took anything or ate.

The infection, and Mum's refusal to take the required medicine, was obviously worrying, but the bigger diagnosis was much more frightening. Her behaviour was clearly symptomatic of more serious delirium. Not dementia, which I knew she had always feared as Dad had feared cancer, but a severe medical condition in itself. Her growing paranoia, card fixation, moments of extreme anxiety, and emotional and mental fluctuations were all typical of the condition. Whilst I didn't want to hear any of this, I couldn't deny it, and I understood the situation. Unfortunately, it seemed to make sense. Despite Mum still saying she wasn't ill, she must have known somewhere in her mind that things weren't right. Her focus on cards and bridge, things she had been so good at in the past, were surely her subconscious attempt and struggle to get things back under control.

As the days went on, despite moments of clarity, Mum's condition did not seem to be improving. The doctors said that while there were ways to get the infection under control, the delirium was more difficult to gauge. It could take days, weeks, months, or even longer.

Conversations started about options for Mum to move to specialist care facilities at some point, but for now, we needed to wait a little longer before putting anything in place. This was a scenario I had not been prepared for. What about Dad? He couldn't live on his own at the house if Mum was away, despite daily visits from the carer. And he wouldn't want to. I doubted whether he would be able to go anywhere with Mum, and I didn't want him to go to a different home himself. Also I would have to go back to work at some point; I needed the income. I decided I wouldn't think about it. My priority was the here and now.

The first thing Dad asked about when I got back was Mum, understandably. I needed to protect him though. I wanted to be honest, but I never was completely, holding back some of the bleaker developments. I used to tell him Mum was able to laugh, had been asking about him, and was pleased to hear he was coping relatively well. She missed him and wanted to come home, but it was early days, and she still seemed quite preoccupied with the cards. I did tell him about the delirium but probably didn't say how serious it was or what might be the longer-term implications.

Friends were very kind and supportive when I updated them. Katie, now living near her daughter in Wiltshire, called me every evening. She and Mum had spoken on the phone every day, and they had built up a good friendship over the fifty years they had been neighbours.

Working from home and going back and forth to the hospital meant I could shop for Dad and make sure we had hot meals. He no longer listened to his talking books or music, and he wasn't able to see the television. But we used to talk about the news, check share prices, anything to try and keep a sense of normality. He was grateful to see visitors as always. Eva, who was Mum and Dad's cleaner for many years, and Darren who helped with the garden and odd jobs, came round still, and neighbours popped in. Fionulla included.

Nolan and I had booked tickets to see Diana Rigg in conversation at the Royal Festival Hall on Saturday 9 March. I'd spoken to Mum and Dad about it, and we had recalled the old *Avengers* days. Despite Mum's situation now, Dad wanted me to go, so we thought about how we could manage it if Mum wasn't around to look after Dad. Luckily, the carer agreed to stay overnight on the Saturday, with me coming back on the Sunday morning before lunch, after calling in on Mum on the way. The carer, in her way, had been good to Mum and Dad over the last few years, and we trusted her to stay a night. And we knew she would also appreciate the extra money the night shift would bring.

On the Saturday afternoon, I left Dad dozing in the knowledge the carer would arrive shortly and drove to the hospital. Mum had been moved to a more general part of the ward. When I got there, she was sitting in the chair by her bed, in one of her favourite cardigans which I had taken in, laughing away with the assistant who was on duty to mind her. This was a good sign I thought, although I knew it was no indication of any significant or permanent improvement as yet. We were able to chat relatively normally, and I told her about my planned evening and how Dad was being looked after. She actually seemed quite happy, and apart from badly needing to get her hair done, looked much brighter. Before I left, I again told her to eat, drink, and take the tablets I had "brought in" from her doctor. I had taken in some cakes to encourage her. With her still in the chair, I said, 'I love you. Now you behave yourself, and I'll see you tomorrow.' She laughed and said to anyone in earshot, 'Did you hear what he just said?' Pointing at me, still laughing, she said, 'Well you behave yourself.' I left to drive back to the flat.

I left the car at the Westfield car park in Stratford and walked back to the flat. It was such a relief to be back for a bit, even if it was only going to be for one night in my own bed again. I put some smart clothes on, which felt nice, and Nolan and I went up to town. We saw Diana Rigg, who was very entertaining, had a few drinks, and finished with a meal out afterwards. It had been good to spend time with Nolan and be able to go out again. I felt quite reassured that both Mum and Dad were comfortable and being looked after while I was away.

At around four thirty on the Sunday morning, my mobile woke me. It was the hospital. A doctor told me that Mum had taken a turn for the worst and asked if I could get to the hospital as soon as possible, and he would meet me to explain. Nolan heard the call from his bedroom next door and knew I was up. We booked a taxi to take me to the hospital rather than walk back to Stratford to get my car. It arrived quickly. I can't remember what I was thinking on the journey over, which thankfully didn't take long at that time of day.

The hospital was basically shut, but I found someone who told me how to get up to the ward through the basement and staff lifts. The doctor was waiting for me when I got to the ward. He seemed to be the only person on duty. He took me to a side room and told me to sit down. I remember telling him to tell me everything.

He explained that shortly before he had called me, Mum had suffered a severe brain haemorrhage while sleeping. It had been unexpected, quick, and she would not have known or experienced any pain. Someone had been with her when it happened, and he had been on duty on that ward. He said there were now three likely outcomes. The first was that she would come round and recover at some point. The second was that she would recover some degree of consciousness but would show signs of brain damage which would probably be long-lasting. The third outcome was that she would not recover at all and would not survive. I asked what he really thought. He said that because intervention of any sort would not help or be possible, particularly given Mum's age, it was his opinion that it was unlikely that Mum would survive. I mentioned that Mum had fallen and hit her head on her first night there and asked if that had contributed or brought it on. He said it wouldn't have. Unfortunately, it was a case of someone just reaching their time to go. I asked how long Mum might have. He said he thought she didn't have long. I seem to remember I cried, but somehow, practicalities seemed to take over. Immediately I thought of Dad and what I was going to have to tell him.

The doctor took me to see Mum. She was in the same ward as the night before. She lay on the bed, eyes closed, and looked as though she was fast asleep, although I knew it was more than that. She looked peaceful. She had just one drip going into her arm, which I was told was a painkiller. Mum, as well as Dad, had specified long before that they weren't to be resuscitated should anything happen, a choice I felt I had to honour however hard it was now that such a situation had arisen. Quality of life was also important, so even if Mum did pull through physically but had permanent brain damage, unlikely though this was, I knew she would not have wanted to live like that. The doctor told me they were no longer giving her liquids. She looked peaceful and was breathing quietly and easily, her mouth slightly open. I spoke to her, kissed her, and sat holding her hand. She was totally unresponsive.

There was nothing I could do. It was going to be a case of watching and waiting. The doctor felt that we had some time. Knowing I needed to be with Dad, he suggested I go back to my home, do what I needed to do to prepare for the worst whilst I could, and then return to the hospital to see how things were before heading home to be with Dad.

I called for a car to get me and called Nolan whilst I waited. I've no recollection now of how I felt or what I was thinking about. I hope I wasn't thinking selfishly.

I went straight to Stratford, collected my car, and then drove to the flat. I talked to Nolan, who was concerned for me as much as for anyone else, then drove back to the hospital. The doctor I had seen had finished his shift, but I was able to speak to nurses and another doctor. They were straightforward and practical, but empathetic. Some of them I recognised from previous visits. Nothing seemed to have changed. Mum was "sleeping" peacefully. A nurse cleared and moistened her mouth, but she was breathing without difficulty. She looked younger, her skin clear. Her hair by now was straighter and longer. I held her hand, she was warm. I spoke to her for a while, kissed her, told her we loved her, and said I was going to see Dad and then come back later. She would have wanted to know that Dad was being looked after.

Outside, I sat and thought about what I was going to say to Dad. I had to keep him calm and stable. I had to take charge. I decided to tell him nothing new. Anything I said now would shock and distress him beyond belief. We had not seen this coming at all, and I didn't know how he would hold up, being frail himself. It was always assumed Dad would go first. He had never remotely thought about life without Mum. He would, obviously, take it badly. He would want to go and see Mum now but would not be able to, and that would destroy him. I decided I would wait and tell him the worst when and if it finally happened. I think I had accepted it was going to happen.

Before I got into the car, I think I called Jennifer and Fionulla. I didn't know what opportunity I would have to call when I got home in case I was in earshot of Dad. I think I wanted to see if they agreed with my decision to hold back from Dad.

Dad was comfortable when I got there, and the night with me away had been quite successful. I told him I had just come from the hospital and would probably go back later. I told him there hadn't been much change, but that I had been able to get through to Mum a bit, and we had been able to talk and laugh, all of which had been true the night before. Dad and I had lunch and carried on as usual. When he was sleeping, I was able to make some more calls from the garden and let the neighbours know. I explained how I was protecting Dad and the approach I was taking with him, and they thought I was doing the right thing.

The carer arrived in the evening. I told her the news but said how important it was that Dad didn't know and should be cared for as normal, which I know must have been hard for her, as she was as fond of Mum as she was of Dad. I went back to the hospital to see Mum, thinking it could be for the last time. If the end was coming and Mum was never going to regain consciousness or any glimmer of recognition, I had made up my mind, rightly or wrongly, that I would prefer not to be there when it happened. Now would be the time to say what I wanted to.

Mum looked the same as earlier. No distress, no sign of pain. The doctor on duty said it wouldn't be much longer now. I had taken a photograph of the family from Mum and Dad's fortieth wedding anniversary celebration, and I placed it on her pillow so that she had us all near. I put a pack of her own bridge cards on the bed.

I held her hand, so small and fragile. I smoothed her hair and stroked her face. How I hoped for a reaction, however small, but none came, so I knew we were nearing the end. I had heard from somewhere that we didn't know whether someone in Mum's condition could hear or not, but hoping Mum could, I sat and talked to her. I remember saying how wonderful she was to both Dad and me, the best wife, the best mother, taking care not to make it seem final or in the past tense. I talked of the family, our holidays, the garden, friends, my flat, and how much Dad missed her and wanted her home. Above all, I told her how much Dad and I loved her. I think I talked to her for about two hours. I hope she heard. If she had, she would have thought I was being sentimental or sloppy, but I am like my mother emotionally, so I know how much my words would have meant to her.

When I felt I had said everything I wanted to, and knowing I could do no more, I took Mum's wedding and engagement rings off her finger. I couldn't remember ever seeing her without them on. I kissed her, hugged her, had a small cry, and told her I loved her again.

I thanked the staff on the ward for what they were doing and left. Back home, I told Dad that Mum was stable and sleeping.

Dad was prepared for the night, and he went to sleep quickly. *Thank goodness*, I thought. I updated Nolan and apart from going up to check on Dad throughout the night, I stayed awake downstairs, not able to sleep. I was expecting the hospital to call at any moment. I called my cousin Caroline in California, the time difference making it possible to talk properly in the middle of the night. Caroline as always was so kind and had gone through something like this herself with her dad, Cousin John. I didn't hear from the hospital.

In the morning, Dad woke. I made tea and called the hospital. No change. Mum was hanging on; she was strong physically, but the scenario was the same. The carer arrived, I updated her, and decided I would go back to see Mum again. Of course, Dad would have wondered why I hadn't gone if I had just stayed home.

When I got there, everything was as it had been the night before. I talked a bit but wasn't really sure what more I could say, if anything. I felt I didn't want to dilute the sentiments I had already expressed with trivialities. I wanted my final words to be meaningful. I didn't stay too long. What was the point? The longer I stayed, the more the image of her just lying there would be imprinted on my mind. That was not how I wanted to remember and visualise my mum.

I carried on as best I could for the rest of the day, waiting for the call, and updating family and friends when Dad was asleep and couldn't hear. I continued to work from home as I had done since I had been with Dad. I had kept up to date with my emails, answered calls, and responded to queries from my colleagues which had continued to come through. The carer came as usual, so Dad was looked after.

Again I didn't sleep that night, or the next. I didn't go back to the hospital again, although Dad thought I was going daily. I walked up to the shops instead, calling people on the way with updates, and returning when I thought my absence tallied with the time it would have taken for a hospital trip. Jennifer went in to see Mum, as did Fionulla and Sue. Nothing had changed. They found Mum to be as I had left her, calm and peacefully lying in bed. I am so grateful to them for going to see Mum; it shows how much she was loved. As the days went by, I did feel guilty at times for not going back, but I had done and said all I could, and I wanted to preserve our last time together as being special. And I was expecting a call at any time.

Late in the evening of Thursday 14 March, long after Dad had gone to sleep, Fionulla called. She was at the hospital with Mum. Mum had just passed away. It had happened. My first reaction was gratitude that Mum hadn't been alone and that it had been quick and painless. One final, slightly deeper breath, and that was it. As Fionulla spoke, I happened to be sitting directly in front of family photographs and was looking at Mum. It then hit me. Has she really gone? She can't have. It felt odd. Real but unimaginable. I had been expecting it, but now that it had happened, I realised I hadn't experienced anything like this before. I found it hard to accept. Fionulla said she would come round, and she arrived shortly afterwards, bringing the photograph and cards with her. Dad was still fast asleep upstairs; I decided not to wake him yet. We had a drink and talked quietly for a bit, which really helped me. She said some wonderful things about Mum, all said with genuine affection.

My thoughts turned to Dad; he was my priority. I decided I would wait and tell him in the morning, when he had some strength as he would need it. Late at night, now, was not the right time. I didn't know how I would do it, or exactly what I would say. It would be the worst thing I would ever have to do. We agreed that I would let the carer get Dad up and give him breakfast first, before I told him on my own. Fionulla very kindly said she would come round and be there to see Dad immediately after, to support me, and to try and give Dad some comfort with the fact that Mum had gone peacefully. I decided I would tell Dad straight but distort the truth and timings slightly. I would say Fionulla had just come from the hospital, where she had been with Mum, who had been sleeping soundly. Mum had then taken a breath and suffered a fatal brain haemorrhage, quickly, with no knowledge of it, and without feeling any pain. Not completely untrue, but hopefully gentler and maybe a bit easier for him to come to terms with.

After Fionulla had gone, I sat quietly and wept. I tried not to cry for myself but probably did. I wasn't angry, but I felt sad and to a degree, bereft and alone. I remember I struggled to use or accept the words "death", "dying", or "died" in relation to my mother. They seemed too brutal, too final. But nothing seemed appropriate. "Passing", "leaving", "going", "no longer with us" were no better.

It seemed to take ages for morning to come. Dad had a good, comfortable night, and I hadn't needed to speak to him as he hadn't woken. So I had just sat downstairs. When it did come, I carried on as usual. I made the tea. I think I called Nolan and maybe a few others as Dad and I waited for the carer to arrive for her first visit. I told her what had happened. She was upset, but I told her I needed her help to get Dad up and fed as normal. While she was looking after Dad upstairs, Fionulla arrived. I was so grateful to have her there.

The carer came back downstairs. I took a deep breath and went up. Dad was sitting upright. I took his hand and said, 'Dad, can you hear me? It's bad news, but I'm with you. Fionulla is here and has just come back from seeing Mum in the hospital.' I was barely able to get it out, but did.

'What?' he cried. 'She's dead? No! No!' He broke down, and I held him close. 'She's left us! No!' He sobbed. I don't remember how long we stayed like that, both of us holding each other and crying.

Fionulla, bless her, came into the room and very calmly and

gently told Dad how she had been there, how Mum had not suffered, how it had been quick, and how calm, ladylike, and peaceful Mum had looked. 'She was always a lady,' she said.

'She was,' said Dad.

I know Fionulla and the carer both left soon after, and I saw them talking to the neighbours outside. I then went back up to Dad. Whilst devastated and in disbelief, I could see he was trying to be as strong as he could for me. But it couldn't have been easy. 'Don't leave me,' he pleaded. I assured him I wouldn't. We sat crying and talking for a while. I needed to let it out after the last few days of covering up the reality and trying to carry on, but I remember thinking I had been right to keep Dad as protected from the details as best I could.

Somehow, Dad became practical. 'There will be a lot to do,' he said. 'We need to let people know.' I said I would take care of everything with him. A few years before, Mum and Dad had both agreed for the London Anatomy Office to look after them after they had gone. This was something Norman had done. From my parents' point of view, this meant they could give something back, avoid extortionate funeral or cremation costs, but more important, leave me with one less thing to organise. Ideally Dad and I should have been left to ourselves that dreadful Friday, but there were things I had to do almost immediately. In a way, this helped give me something to focus on.

I had to notify the Anatomy Office quickly as I knew there would be a time frame involved. I called and they couldn't have been kinder or more understanding. They told me what I had to do and what paperwork they would need. Geraldine and Jennifer also explained the process I needed to go through. I booked an appointment for the following Tuesday to register Mum at the registry office in Enfield.

The hospital had Mum's paperwork already, but I was told a coroner would have to see her to issue the certificate since she had not seen her own doctor within the last two weeks. They said that might not be until Monday. In the end, it became a race against time to try and meet the four-day deadline set by the Anatomy Office. The certificate did come through on the Monday, so I had everything I needed to take to the registry office. Jennifer recommended getting plenty of copies of the death certificate, which I would need and did end up using.

We missed the four-day deadline required for London, but the Anatomy Office was able to accept Mum in Wales. How ironic. Mum loved Wales after so many happy holidays and visits there, and now she was going back again. Dad was pleased. In time, there will be a cremation and thanksgiving service for donors' families in Cardiff, and Mum's ashes will then come back to me.

That weekend, after the awful Friday, Dad and I talked a lot. Between tears we were able to talk about Mum, remembering all the good times and some of the bad. I felt so sorry for him, lying there in poor health himself, without Mum by his side. After seventy-one years together. It must have been awful. I told Dad about the arrangements, and we talked of getting a small tree for my eventual garden under which Mum, and then when the time came Dad, could be placed so that we would all be together.

With some calls made and neighbours informed, word about Mum spread, and we started to get cards and flowers. Over the following weeks, Dad got a lot of comfort from me reading all the cards again and again with their wonderful memories and anecdotes of Mum. She was well loved by many.

As we wouldn't be arranging a funeral or cremation ourselves,

Dad wanted to have some sort of religious acknowledgement, so on the Sunday, I went up to St Paul's church to see if I could meet the vicar, Father Daniel. I met him, and he was so kind, although none of us had been regular churchgoers for some time. I found it difficult talking, sobbing of course. In fact, I was to practically lose my voice for the next two weeks, some sort of shock I suppose. I asked if he would come and see Dad, and he did on the Thursday. We said prayers, which was lovely. Dad cried, as he had done regularly since the Friday before. Father Daniel asked him what Mum was like and what he remembered. 'Kind, she was so kind,' Dad said. Prayers were said for Mum in church on the following Sunday.

As well as going to the registry office, I had other things to arrange. I had sent a brief text to my bosses at work and hoped I could be spared any further work duties whilst I looked after Dad and put things in order. I knew I would have to return to the office at some stage, but that would have to wait. In the event, the company was very supportive. Geraldine came over for a day to help me sort all the paperwork out, knowing what to do since she had done it all for Norman not too long before. Jennifer also offered to write any letters that might be needed. Mum's control of household affairs and finances made things quite straightforward, but we found so much paperwork in drawers, cupboards, and wardrobes upstairs and down. I had been Mum's power of attorney, but, of course, that had now stopped. As we thought Dad would go before Mum, everything, apart from joint ownership of the house, had been in Mum's name— savings, shares, pensions, and all bills. Dad had no more than about £5,000 to his name. I was able to transfer some things over but had to arrange probate for everything else, and all monies subsequently had to be frozen. Luckily I had some savings so could draw on those to ensure bills were paid.

I was able to get back to the flat that first week to collect things, see Nolan, and get some notecards from Westfield. I didn't know when I would be able to go back again properly. Also that week, Caroline happened to be over from California, and she and Gordon travelled up to town, and with Nolan, came out for dinner in Stratford. I needed to see her, and we had a lovely evening, laughing at the memories we shared. I gave her Mum's scarves to share with Angela.

About a week later, my friend John, who I had known since 1982 when we met at Harrods, held a party in Covent Garden to celebrate his sixtieth birthday. I wasn't really feeling up to it but wanted to try and go. Dad encouraged me, so I went, and it was a much-needed tonic. I hope I wasn't too self-indulgent or come across as feeling sorry for myself. People I have known for as long as John were there, and we had all shared a lot of good times. Marian and Richard, Geraldine, Carlos and James, Judy and Pete, Bill and Liz, Tracey, Emma, Sue and Charlie, Marilyn and Julian, Paul and Tina, and Ann and Peter among them. Many had lost parents themselves, John included. And Tracey and Sue had suffered family tragedies which had been much worse. The evening reminded me how life goes on.

Seeing Caroline and going to John's celebration were only possible because of the carer's support.

As well as notifying some people by phone, mostly immediate family, and telling neighbours, I preferred to write. Dad and I went through Mum's address books, and I think I was able to get to everyone, but some people were missed. It wasn't until last Christmas that I tracked everyone down as cards arrived to 'Jose and Len'.

As Dad couldn't get out of bed, we arranged to have people to the house to remember Mum but also to see Dad. We decided on Sunday 19 May. Everyone I could think of or who had sent wishes were invited and most confirmed. Around thirty-five people in total. I made an invitation card from us both showing a scene of poppies. Mum loved poppies and had a number of prints, although she was never successful growing them in the garden with such hard, clay soil.

Whilst I continued to sort Mum's affairs out, I stayed with Dad, sleeping in Mum's bed. The carer and Eva came as usual, and I tried to keep things going as Mum would have done. I could hear Mum telling us to eat and drink and keep healthy. Dad had three meals a day and ate well. I shopped, talked to friends and family, tidied the house as Mum would have done, put the bins out, and so on. Darren and I looked after the garden. I wasn't ready to look at Mum's things, so everything was cleaned if needed and put away.

Dad and I sat and spoke a lot. I knew a lot about the Kirbys, probably because I had known so many of them, but not so much about Dad. As well as talk about Mum, Dad talked about his childhood a lot. His mother had a sister who lived on the Isle of Wight, married to a gamekeeper. Dad and his brothers and sisters used to go there for holidays, spending time with cousins I had never been aware of. Dad talked of rowing on the River Lee, playing on Hackney Marshes, and of Reg, Joan, and Norma. It was good to fill in a number of gaps.

Friends came round to see Dad, including Fionulla, Jill, and various other neighbours. And we had calls from well-wishers and a constant stream of cards. Dad and I called his niece, Denise. Dad hadn't spoken or written to Denise for quite some time, and I hadn't seen or talked to her for years. When we spoke, Denise thought I sounded just like Dad. It meant a lot to Dad to speak. Denise was one of the only Pugh family members left. If they could, Denise and her husband, David, said they would be there at the house in May.

On the 4 April, for what would have been Mum and Dad's sixty-third wedding anniversary, I bought some flowers and cards for them both, and Dad and I had a toast. We did the same for Mum's birthday on 18 April. Mum would have been ninety-one.

# Chapter 3

## DAD

As I got in control of Mum's affairs, I was able to resume work and catch up, but working from home could not continue indefinitely. I would need to go back to the office and hopefully start getting back to the flat. However, Dad was the priority. I wanted to do everything I could to look after him as Mum had done, and more important, let him know I would always be there for him. He was very brave as the weeks went by but missed Mum terribly, even though I was there. We talked about what we might be able to do. He wanted to remain at home, and although he and Mum had talked about residential care if it came to it, neither of us gave it serious thought; it still would be a last resort. As well as two visits a day from the carer, brief at times with the children in tow, we did have visits from district nurses and doctors as required. But Dad couldn't be left alone for long, and it wouldn't have been feasible for him to come and live with me if I was out at work. It would have been too much of a change for him anyway, and living on the fifth floor of a small flat would not have worked. Dad was willing to consider and try anything though to enable me to get home and back to work but allow him to stay in The Spinney.

We spoke to the carer and came up with a plan which we thought might work. I would spend three days at the flat and go back to work from there and then stay with Dad for the other four days and nights, again working from home which had worked quite well. When I wasn't with Dad, the carer would make four visits during the day rather than two, and her mother, supplemented by a few ex-NHS carers in her circle, would stay the relevant nights. We knew this wasn't ideal, but after a negotiation of rates, we agreed to try it. I also arranged for Dad to have a panic button, which when triggered would alert me, Darren, and the carer, and go through to a central support centre that would have a key to the house.

I set up a spare bed for the carer in the upstairs front room and confirmed that I would leave all of Dad's meals and food in the house so he would be fed well. He had a mobile with him as well as the panic button, so he could contact me at any time if I wasn't there, and I would call him regularly.

It took a while to adapt to this arrangement, and I couldn't relax for the first week. But Dad and I were determined to make it work if we could. It was good to get home to the flat and sleep in my own bed in my own room again. I was able to catch up with friends. My friend Beth came round and listened to my woes of the horrendous past months. She was wonderful, as was Nolan and his mother, Debi, who called regularly.

I returned to work, and in addition to my usual duties, was given a substantial associate recruitment campaign to run. Adverts had already been placed with our recruitment partner, and it meant I would be required to develop application assessment criteria, acknowledge and screen all applicants, hold telephone interviews, make notes, shortlist, reject, book fuller interviews, and answer questions. It was a substantial piece of work and would be time consuming, but it was something I could do easily from either the office or home.

It wasn't long before Dad and I recognised the arrangements we had put in place weren't really working, although Dad didn't want to complain. He wanted me to have a life, and he didn't want to be a burden, which he would never have been. It transpired that the carer was unreliable during the day, and at night, the carers weren't particularly attentive. I was often called by the panic support team when Dad couldn't get a response from them, even though they were in the house. Neighbours who visited showed concern, and Darren called me to say he was worried, although he knew the carer well.

Before we had time to look at a possible alternative arrangement, matters were taken out of our hands. On 26 April, Dad, always prone to infections, developed another one and needed hospitalisation. He had been in discomfort in the morning, and the carer had noticed a rash on his leg. Luckily I was there. As the morning progressed, he became disorientated. After a visit from the doctor, Dad was taken to North Middlesex Hospital once again. His condition was recognised immediately, and he was admitted for observation and medication, to remain at least until the infection disappeared, however long that might be.

I informed my company, having to say again I wouldn't be able to get in. I had made up my mind to see Dad every day he was in hospital. I would not leave him, as he had asked. So this time I told my company that given the circumstances, I would resign and leave once the recruitment campaign was complete. That should take no longer than a month. The company was very supportive; they didn't apparently want to lose me, so they suggested I take a six-month unpaid sabbatical once the campaign had finished. I agreed without much thought.

I visited Dad daily. Nolan came with me to visit, meeting Dad for the first time. I had left my car at The Spinney, so I went to the hospital each day by train. I would get up at five o'clock each morning and start work. I went to the hospital around eleven, and then come home to work into the evening. I didn't eat well. I often had to conduct telephone interviews on the way to the hospital and back, or even at the hospital itself. And I was also going home to The Spinney to make sure the house was secure and in good order. I didn't have time to think about meals.

It took time for Dad to begin to get over the infection, but once again, he was fighting back. He was so pleased to see me each day as he wasn't happy there. He hated the food, missed Mum, and wasn't able to sleep much in the noisy ward. We were having a period of good weather, and his bed was by the window. He was too hot and uncomfortable. I was able to speak to various members of staff, when I could find them, and they felt that whilst Dad was recovering, he should be kept under further observation as his heart rate was irregular, and his blood pressure was up. As soon as Dad did appear to show signs of recovery, he caught one new infection after another, which totally depressed him. It was at this point he said that when he did get out, he would need a different sort of care, more constant and monitored. He said he felt he should go into care. I privately agreed but wanted to make certain he was sure, so I didn't push it. However, without Mum to get home to, he was decided.

I spoke to Geraldine to find out more about the residential home Jean was in. How wonderful if Dad could go there with her. We would have to pay for it, as owning a house meant Dad did not qualify for any support. I could use my savings whilst we waited for probate. Dad seemed enthusiastic, and it was arranged for nurses to come from Jean's home to visit him in hospital to assess whether they would be able to take him. They felt they could and had room, but given Dad was bedbound, said they would need Dad to be able to stand unaided on his own, a big challenge, before moving him in. The nurses arranged for Jignash, their physiotherapist, to come and see Dad to determine whether this was at all possible and how long it might take if it was. Dad was so positive when Jignash assessed him. He really wanted to try and stand again, and he was ready to work as hard as he could in order to achieve it. He said the thought had given him a new lease on life, and we said how pleased Mum would be. I was so proud of him and told him so.

Jignash felt that there was a seven out of ten chance Dad would stand again, but it would take time given Dad's inactivity for well over a year. Luckily, there was no damage to his legs, only muscle wastage. It meant though that Dad would have to wait until going to join Jean. We would need to find somewhere else for him to be while he underwent physiotherapy. Jignash was so helpful, recommending an alternative care and residential home in Southgate. It was more than likely they would take Dad if they had a free room. I called Beatrice, the manager there, and with Jignash's recommendation, she agreed to take him. Nolan and I went to see the Southgate Beaumont, based in a wonderful old building near The Cherry Tree. We knew the place well; Mum and Dad had both visited friends when they stayed there in the past. In a way, it was like a hotel. When I told Fionulla, she said it was very well regarded and had a good reputation.

Getting Dad there was frustrating as new infections kept coming.

But he eventually recovered enough to get moved on Saturday 18 May, the day before Mum's memorial at home. I hoped he would never have to go back to that hospital again. Dad was so relieved to get there. The room was bright and seemed comfortable. He had a freshly cooked food menu to choose from, and Beatrice and the staff were very welcoming. He would be monitored constantly, and full medical facilities were on site if needed. After what seemed to have been months, I felt Dad would be properly looked after now, and it proved to be the case.

Dad wanted me to go ahead with Mum's memorial, but it meant that no one would be able to pay their respects to Dad personally since he wouldn't be at home. Dad was disappointed but accepted it and knew that people would be visiting him at the Beaumont. He was just excited about being looked after properly and working with Jignash.

In the days before the Sunday, Dad and I had been planning Mum's memorial. I made sure the downstairs of the house was just as Mum used to keep it—tidy, clean, and free of any medical equipment. I bought loads of flowers and had ordered food and drink from Waitrose to be delivered on the Sunday morning. Jennifer was making and bringing one of Mum's favourite cakes. The garden looked beautiful, just as Mum would have wanted. I stayed at The Spinney the night before, knowing I could leave Dad to settle in and get used to his new room. He was exhausted after the move and had been keen to sleep. On the Sunday morning, Jennifer and Nolan came early to help me set up. We put the food out on the dining table using all of Mum's best china and cutlery. Drink was in the kitchen. Tables and chairs had been set out in the garden.

Everyone who could have been there was: Nolan, the family, our friends, various neighbours, and even Sue from the hairdressers. My cousin Denise and David managed to get there, which was nice. As I opened the door to her, it was like looking at Dad's mother, my nana Edith, or his sister Norma, Denise's mother, neither of whom I had seen for what must have been thirty years. But Denise looked so familiar and recognisable. I told Dad the next day.

I think the memorial went well. Mum would have been so pleased and no doubt surprised at the number of people there. I do hope she knew how much she was loved. I think I held it together. I made a speech and talked of Dad as well as Mum. I can't remember exactly what I said, but it seemed to flow. Someone filmed it on their phone. I was tearful, of course, but managed to crack a few jokes. I am a Kirby after all. We played the hymn we knew Mum had wanted—"Make Me a Channel of Your Peace"—in versions by Katherine Jenkins and one of her favourites, Aled Jones.

The memorial lasted about three hours. Nolan and I tidied up and went home before going out for dinner. I had promised to visit and update Dad the next day. Nolan said he was proud of me, which meant a lot.

I went to see Dad the next day, the Monday. I took some photos and things for his room, even though we were hoping it was just going to be a temporary stay. Dad had begun work with Jignash that morning, and with my news from the day before, he seemed positive. He told me I had done a good job. We went through the menu for the week ahead, and I think Dad was surprised at what was offered. Like Mum, he did like good food.

Over the coming weeks, I went to see him at least every other day. Nolan and I were able to get away for a few days to Deal, but that was the only time he was left for more than a day without seeing me. He worked hard each day with Jignash and was able to start moving his legs. He had visitors, and he was animated, asking about friends and family. We talked a lot about work, which he was pleased to hear I was finishing for a while, my flat, the friends I had seen, football—which I don't know much about—and the farce that was Brexit.

One day Jennifer suggested we should try and get Jean over to visit Dad. They had not seen each other for a few years, but I had taken Mum to visit Jean in her residential home a few times, and they had spoken as much as possible on the phone in the months before Mum was taken ill. Mum and Dad had known Jean and Norman since moving to The Vale in 1956, a long time for a friendship.

Jennifer and I were able to get Jean in a chair and in to see Dad. She had been told about Mum, but by now was tending to get confused herself, which was natural, and on the way over, asked a few times whether Mum was still with us. Like the rest of us, she had thought Dad would have been the first. 'What about Len?' she kept asking. We reminded her that she was going to see him now. When we got there, we wheeled her into Dad's room and up to the bed. She took his hand. 'Hello Len', she said. 'Are you happy?' He said no and cried. I had never heard him actually say this before, and I felt so sorry for him. It had nothing to do with me. Dad repeatedly said how he appreciated everything I was doing, and he was doing all he could to support me. But nothing would replace Mum. He had loved her so much, and she had been there with him every day, through good and bad, for all that time.

We spent a while in the room, letting Jean and Dad reminisce about old times. I'm so glad we got them together. And although we said we would do it again, it never happened.

Not long after getting to the Beaumont, Dad announced he felt he should sell The Spinney. He was hoping and planning to recover enough strength to move to Jean's residential home, and he realised he would never go home again given the care and support he would need. I asked him if he was sure, and he was. 'But for a good price,' he said. Although we were still waiting for Mum's probate to come through, we had been able to transfer the house solely to Dad, and I had been made power of attorney for him, too, so I would be able to set things in motion for him if he were to sell. Our solicitor came to see Dad at the Beaumont, and Dad signed the relevant paperwork to begin.

When I went to see Dad, I always went to the house first to mow the lawn, look after the garden, put the bins out, clean the windows, and make sure the place looked lived in and tidy. Basically I wanted it to be as Mum and Dad had enjoyed it. As a result, it was practically ready to go on the market. But first I stacked all of Dad's medical equipment into the garage, arranged for his hospital bed to be returned, and paid for the stair lift to be collected. Upstairs could then be reconfigured and arranged back to a normal bedroom and living space. The house needed a bit of painting, but given all new owners have their own ideas for redecoration, I left that. I tried everywhere to give away the medical equipment—walking frames, chairs, bath supports, and such—but I couldn't get rid of it. I tried hospitals, care homes, hospices, and charities. In the end, my friends Martin and Peter came over with their van, and we cleared everything from the garage and took it all to the local skip. Such a waste.

June was probably the wrong time to sell as holidays were approaching, but we went ahead with the valuation, agreed on a fair and reasonable price for marketing, and put it up for sale. 'So goodbye to The Spinney,' Dad said. At every visit, Dad asked whether we had sold but told me to wait and only accept a decent offer however long that may take. He didn't want it going cheap. We talked about what would happen when we did sell. Both Mum and Dad knew I was thinking of retiring to Deal in Kent at some point. We had spoken about how, if Mum was alone when I did, perhaps she could come too and have a small flat on her own near me. 'I don't want to live with you,' she said. Laughing, but actually meaning it. Now, even though Dad moving to Jean's residential home was still the plan. Dad and I talked about how Dad might use the sale money and buy somewhere in Deal in his name now, which I could live in and inherit later. Nolan had even suggested finding a local care home for Dad down there. Dad was quite open to it all. 'A new phase,' he said.

Dad seemed to settle well at the Beaumont. He felt looked after and liked the fact that now, free from work, I could visit easily. He worked hard with Jignash and showed me how he could move his legs. He got to know the staff and was able to joke with them, and even tell them off on occasion, which they took well. He wasn't being serious though and didn't complain. Although he thought of and missed Mum constantly, he was giving things a go. I was relieved; the care was obviously working, and infections seemed to be a thing of the past.

Whilst things seemed positive on the whole, I did begin to notice very slight changes as we got further into June. Dad was comfortable at first and remained alert, asking about the house; what I'd been up to; how Nolan, Beth, and the family were; who I had spoken to; and what had been happening in the world. He was always pleased to see people when they visited, particularly Fionulla and her children. We had settled into a new kind of routine, although both of us still expected his time there to be relatively temporary, until he could get to Jean. My visits were never too long as Dad got tired, especially after his physiotherapy in the mornings; he always slept in the afternoons after lunch anyway. But he began to want to sleep more often, and while able to talk about everyday things, he started asking where his mother was and how Reg was. He asked if I was staying the night and if Mum was out. He began to have vivid, detailed dreams, not always happy ones. Most of them related in some way to childhood surroundings. Physically he was doing all right, but mentally, he appeared to drift and become confused. At first I contradicted things he was saying to correct him, but after a while, I learnt not to. I started to just listen and then try and steer him back. The nurses were always attentive and said that this type of behaviour wasn't uncommon and shouldn't cause concern.

I talked to Jignash a lot to see how he was finding Dad. Sadly, although Dad was trying hard and was now able to jiggle around in bed, in Jignesh's professional opinion, it seemed increasingly unlikely that Dad would ever stand again. This meant there was no prospect of him moving to Jean's home or to any residential rather than medical care home. Neither I nor Jignash told Dad this as it was important for Dad to still have a goal, and he was feeling improvement which pleased him greatly.

And so we carried on into July. The house hadn't sold yet, which didn't worry us. I was still maintaining it, and the garden was thriving. Probate still hadn't come through, but with my savings, we were managing. Dad seemed comfortable, well fed, and physically stable. He was clean and well dressed in his own clothes, freshly shaved, and looking bright with a good colour in his face. His hair and nails were looked after. We both enjoyed our time together on my visits, and I always made sure he knew I loved him. When I was younger, I think I thought this was something an adult son shouldn't say to his dad, or any man, but by now, saying it came naturally, and I'm glad I did it. I meant it.

The physiotherapy with Jignash continued. 'Hi, boy', Dad said once when I visited. 'I've been up and went to make a cup of tea, and it wasn't bad. But I'll have another one now.' If Dad thought he was up and about, even though he never would be now, that was no bad thing I decided.

On Monday 22 July, I didn't think Dad looked so well. He had a slight cough, which the nurses said they would keep an eye on. He was able to eat, drink, and swallow though. By the Wednesday, he was talking, and we caught up as we always did. But the nurses said they thought it best to get the doctor to just check on the cough. Whilst pale, he was in quite good spirits. After all, he was used to coughs, colds, and infections. On the Friday, though, he was pretty rough. The doctor had prescribed him an antibiotic to try and shift the cough. He was finding it more difficult to eat and wasn't able to drink much of his tea. He wanted to sleep. I told him I'd be back in the morning but would come back sooner if he wanted me to. He said he could wait. We said goodbye and the usual things. On the way home, I met up with Jennifer and Gordon's son, George, to help him with his CV, and I remember telling him I thought Dad was in a bad way. For some reason, I suddenly felt Dad didn't have too long now. With his general health as it was, and now with a new cough and on antibiotics again, how long could his body keep fighting? When I went to see Dad the next day, Saturday morning, he was sleeping, the effects of the drugs apparently. I didn't stay long; there was no point in waking him as he was breathing quite comfortably. I was told he had eaten his breakfast as usual—two Weetabix with hot milk.

On Sunday 28 July, Nolan and I had been invited to an afternoon birthday party at our neighbours' in the flat opposite. I went to see Dad in the morning. He was asleep again. He didn't look at all well although did not appear to be in distress. I was told the next few days would be quite critical, to check that he didn't develop pneumonia, and the nurses were already monitoring him closely and constantly to see how he was fairing. As power of attorney, I had previously said that unless absolutely necessary, hospital should be avoided. I asked the nurses again to treat Dad for as long as they could at the Beaumont before we thought about moving him. I knew he wouldn't have been able to cope with another trip to hospital, and the nurses agreed. I left him around lunchtime, still sleeping.

When I got back, I told Nolan that I felt things were bad. I went up to our roof and called Veronica and Caroline to say the same thing. I think I also called Fionulla. A few hours later, we made our way over to the neighbours'. I was given a drink. I needed one. After about fifteen minutes, my mobile rang. I couldn't hear properly at first given the noise, but I found a bedroom. It was the Beaumont calling to tell me Dad had just died. It hadn't been five months yet since Mum had gone.

Edie Kirby, my maternal grandmother

Herbert Kirby, my maternal grandfather,
behind the bar at The Woodman

Edie and Herbert with Mum as a baby

The Kirbys - Herbert, Edie, Doll and
John - all dressed up on the Beach

With cousin John's wife Veronica in Little Holland

Herbert and Doll

Mum with Herbert on her right in Hackney Fields

Frederick Pugh, my paternal grandfather

Dad as a boy scout, front row, far right in hat

Dad centre with his brothers, Don on his left, Reg on his right

Dad in his RAF uniform

Dad working in the stock exchange, front row,
far right with pocket handkerchief

Mum on the left with her friend Joy

Dad in a deckchair on a cruise

Mum on an early holiday abroad

Mum's and Dad's wedding. From left, Dad's brother Reg,
their father Frederick, their mother Edith, Dad, Mum,
Winnie and her husband, Mum's brother John

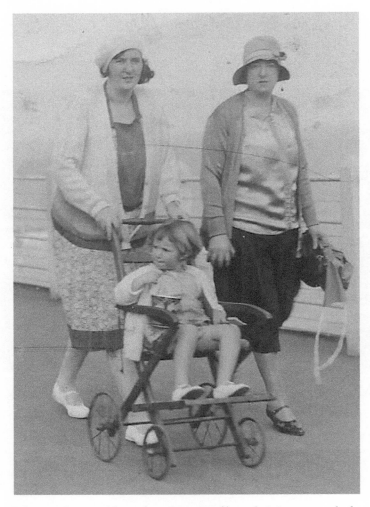

Edie, right, and her daughter Doll with Mum as a baby

Mum, Dad and me at my christening

Dad's mother Edith, my Nana, with me at my christening

Me as baby with Jennifer, left, and Geraldine Tripp

With my cousin John and cousin Janet's
daughter Susie in the garden

Susie and I front right at cousin Stephen's and Lorraine's wedding

Susie and I at cousin John's and Veronica's
wedding, with cousin Stephen on the right

Mum's sisters Gertie and Doll at Mum's and Dad's wedding

Mum, Dad and I on holiday in Wales

The Kirbys at Mum and Dad's 40th – the photo
I left with Mum when she was in hospital

Mum, left, teaching at her Bridge class

Mum on holiday

Dad on holiday

Mum and Dad in Menorca

An 'Andy Warhol' picture of Mum and Dad I
had produced for their 50th Anniversary

Dad at home in The Spinney

Mum at home in The Spinney

Mum and Dad with the Tripps on holiday in France

Mum at her 90th Birthday lunch

Mum's Memorial Invitation

Nolan

Nolan and I

Frankie and I in the house in Deal

Frankie in the sea at Deal, his first time

# ME

I left the party and was back home with Nolan within minutes. We sat on the balcony. I broke down sobbing. I remember having a mixture of thoughts. It was over, and Dad no longer had to fight. I had a sense of relief in a way, but I also felt bereft. I had lost them both. Nolan told his mum, Debi, the news, and she called soon after and said all the right things. The Beaumont had asked whether I wanted to see Dad. I couldn't face it. I had been with him that morning. He had been sleeping, had been alive, and the last thing I had said was that I loved him. I didn't want to see him now, cold and gone, or whatever the stupid word was. I don't think I was being selfish. Arrangements had to be made quickly though. Dad would need to be moved from the home. A doctor had already produced the certificate. Once again I had to call the Anatomy Office, who again showed great kindness. I then called family and Fionulla. Fionulla was wonderful and took over without me asking. She made all the arrangements with a local undertaker to take care of Dad before he could move to the Anatomy Office people. I didn't need to do a thing. I cannot thank Fionulla enough.

In the days that followed, now knowing the procedure, I began arranging things. I was able to collect the death certificate on the Monday and book an appointment with the registry office. Mum and Dad would have smiled. At the registry office, I saw the same person I had seen just months earlier, and I said I hoped she didn't think I was killing off my family. Again there was no burial or cremation. Dad remains in London for the time being. He will be cremated through the Anatomy Office, and then a service will be held in Southwark Cathedral for all those who donated over the rolling year. His ashes will come back to me. Both Mum and Dad will be with me in Deal, beneath that tree we talked about. I think an acer will be nice. With a little plaque.

I did all the relevant paperwork, but this time it frustrated me. I wasn't angry with Dad, but now I just had myself to worry about, and I was exhausted and wanted rid of it all. Mum's probate came through days after Dad went, passing everything to him, so my solicitor has had to begin the whole process again for Dad and Mum together. It's still not finalised.

As with Mum, everyone was so kind. I notified everybody I could think of and received lots of wonderful words and cards. This time I decided not to hold any home memorial for Dad, knowing that those who would want to come will be able to at Southwark when the time comes.

After my unpaid leave from work, I made the decision to resign. I don't miss it other than the people I've had the good fortune to work with. The company held a really nice leaving event for me, and it was nice to see them. I wish them all well.

Shortly after Dad went, I joined the Tripps at Geraldine and Richard's for a garden party for Jean's birthday. We hadn't told Jean about Dad since it hadn't been that long since she'd seen him, and it wouldn't have been the right occasion. As a result, she asked about Dad and also said, 'Jose should have been here.' I will be forever grateful to Jean and her family for their friendship, love, and support to the three of us over so many years.

On November 3, to remember Mum, Father Daniel invited me to the All Souls service at St Paul's. I accepted and let him know about Dad, so both were acknowledged. How Mum and Dad would have laughed to see me in church, and because of them! Amongst the names read out were some I recognised, Mum and Dad's friends of old. My immediate thought was I must tell Mum when I get home.

It's things like that which I find hard. I hear or see things I want to share but can't. That is a tremendous void and always will be, although I know time helps.

The Spinney was sold last September. Of the two offers I had, I accepted the slightly lower one from a young family, the son being only a few years younger than I had been when we moved there back in 1969. Mum and Dad would have been pleased to know their home had been passed on to a family who could build a happy life there and enjoy it as much as we had.

Clearing the house was difficult. Jennifer helped me sort things, particularly Mum's clothes. I kept her wedding and engagement rings and a few sentimental pieces of jewellery that Dad had bought for her over the years. Dad didn't have so much, but I have his watches and medals, his wallet, and a tie from the fifties with a drawing on it which he always said looked like Mum. A lot of things were shared out to the Tripps and family. Mum and Dad would be glad it's being kept. Some items were thrown, some went to charity shops, but I have lots of family pieces, furniture and antiques mostly, including a card table made from Herbert and Edie's bed headboard, and Auntie

Doll's chest of drawers. And of the old cutlery, glass, and china, some of which were wedding presents to them. Nothing particularly valuable but important things for me to have.

The sale of The Spinney took time as we were part of a chain of five which caused no end of frustration. Probate also held things up. Regardless of having to wait, Nolan and I went ahead and made an offer on a period house in Deal, in the conservation area which we wanted, and with the sea at the end of the road. We eventually completed the sale of The Spinney and took ownership of the house in Deal at the end of January this year. The house is seventeenth century, and our plan is to show off its history to its best and decorate and furnish it comfortably but stylishly. It's going to need a bit of work, but we'll enjoy that. Nolan has a very perceptive and creative eye, and I like clutter, so we'll have to make compromises, but we'll get there. Mum and Dad's bits and pieces have been unpacked and found a place alongside our own things. They would be proud.

All being well, we'll be ready to have Nolan's family down to us for Christmas this year. We know where the tree will be going, adorned with all the old family decorations. Last Christmas, Nolan's mum very kindly invited me to join the family down at her house in Dorset. I thought it would be difficult, but being with other people, all so welcoming—Debi, Dan, Tia, Nathan, and Tom, Nanny Shirley, and Nolan of course—helped me a lot.

As a dog walker, Nolan was looking after a neighbour's four-month-old goldendoodle on what turned out to be a daily basis. Frankie. We both loved him from the start, and it seemed he took to us. Over the months that followed, it was Nolan who trained and groomed him, and Frankie would follow him everywhere. He was the perfect puppy. One day Nolan said his owner was going to have to go back to live abroad, and Frankie would need to be re-homed. Although Nolan looked after other dogs, Frankie had become special, and Nolan couldn't bear to think of him moving away to someone new. We offered to take him. In November Frankie came to live with us. It was a totally seamless move, and we wouldn't be without him. He loves life in Deal, although he found a house rather than a small flat a bit confusing at first. He likes to know where we both are, but with three floors and eight rooms, it was obviously a strange and new setup for him. He's very comfortable here now. In a way, he's Nolan's dog first, and his first loyalty is with Nolan. But I know he loves me too. The way he jumps up to greet me and give me a toy whenever I get back from somewhere is very special. I try not to give him too many treats or food from the table, but I do give in. Nolan's more disciplined.

Mum and Dad knew I wanted to get a dog when I had finished working, and they would have adored Frankie.

# Chapter 5

## HERE AND NOW

I am moving on, although my life will never be the same. I know my situation isn't exceptional or unique. What I have been through is nowhere near as tragic as it might have been for others, and I'm grateful for that. Poor Nolan lost his dad at sixty, and we lost Cousin John too early. But kindly meant phrases such as, 'They didn't suffer', 'They had a good life', 'It was a good age', can't take away the fact and sadness of losing my parents.

I still don't think I've been able to grieve properly, and I feel guilty that I haven't, although Nolan says I did. I look back and think I didn't do enough or care enough, but my friend Lee said it is because I did care that I think that, which I hope is true. I certainly did care. Geraldine said to me recently that we should think how both our families were always able to keep our parents close, including them as our lives developed, and that they knew that and appreciated it. How many other families can say the same, having split up or drifted apart? Geraldine and Jennifer always included Mum and Dad in their family occasions, as Jean and Norman had done, and their children, Joanne, Vicky, and George treated them as their own. Jennifer gave Mum and Dad an amaryllis every Christmas, and a homemade cake, which they devoured within days. Our growing blood families always kept Mum and Dad close and in their thoughts, and they all loved them both dearly.

I have days when I have particular moments of sadness. I prefer to be alone when I do to reflect quietly. It comes in waves, though, often at the oddest times. Certain memories, sights and sounds, or music can trigger it. I pray for Mum and Dad every night, as I have always done, but I know they are at peace now. No doubt laughing and arguing in The Woodman Pub, up there on a cloud. But there is often a sense that they are still here but just somewhere else, maybe away for a while or living in The Spinney. I just haven't seen them for a bit.

Each morning, down on the coast, when I listen to the waves breaking, and stop to consider the fresh air and the smells, there is a sense of familiarity. We're back in Broadstairs again. It feels the same. Mum and Dad are here, home with me.

I can still hear their voices and hope I always will. 'Hi boy', Dad says; 'Hi Toots', says Mum. I have messages from them both on my voicemail, but I can't listen to them yet. No doubt the time will come.

I look like Mum; the photos prove it. And hold up a picture of Dad, and I look like him too. I'm proud to be a Kirby, and I'm proud to be a Pugh. I think and hope Mum and Dad were proud of me. In fact, don't worry, Mum and Dad, I know you were.

But like my mother, I am by default insecure and full of self-doubt. Like her, I fill silences with chatter. As an only child I am prepared to be alone and often push others away so that I don't become reliant on them. I expect people to leave me at some point, but I also think the reason I push people away is to test them. To see if they'll come back and show me that they do genuinely like me, thereby restoring a degree of self-worth. However, in public and in company, I have the ability to perform and show the confidence and humour Dad always had. So my two sides merely reflect them both. A true hybrid.

So now, April 2020, we're in lockdown due to the coronavirus pandemic. It's frightening, tragic, and unsettling with many lives already lost. Families and communities have been devastated in far deeper ways than anything I have experienced over this past year. Loved ones have been left behind, and in many cases, they couldn't even say their last goodbyes. Economies are in downturn, and friends are out of work, or "furloughed", not knowing when they can return, if at all. As building work has stopped, our house in Deal is unfinished, and we are restricted to minimal daily exercise outside and only essential trips to join supermarket queues for food. We can't see family or friends, although we Facetime or call. But we carry on knowing a new normal will emerge in time. The Queen rallies us, and we clap or rattle our pans every Thursday evening for the NHS and brave key workers. And we wave to the neighbours. Nolan and I can walk Frankie by the sea or in the fields, keeping a safe distance from passers-by. We are still planning for Christmas, hosting here at the house.

I do wonder whether Mum and Dad would have survived this crisis. Dad would have been extremely vulnerable physically, and Mum would not have coped well in isolation in the house. She would have missed Sue at the hairdressers if nothing else!

Thankfully, as of now, those we know are in good health. Some have contracted the virus along the way but have now fully recovered. I have many good friends, although some—particularly the one and only Trevor Lloyd Jackson, along with Marie-Clare and Nicky from college, James Miller, Julian Rees, Neil from school, and others— have been lost along the way, and I miss them. I would love to hear from them again. I also hope to catch up with Bruce Robertson in America sometime soon. It has been too long.

My wider family remains important to me above all else, and links and regular contact have been and will be maintained. Caroline and Gordon, whilst housebound, are doing well in California. Our trip over for my sixtieth birthday had to be cancelled, but we'll see them again soon. Their sons, Sam and Josh, remain here but are in good spirits, preparing for college. Josh just turned seventeen. Angela and her wife, Lisa, have their beautiful daughter Ottilie. Veronica no doubt will be back travelling again, and hopefully I'll meet Bill when they get back to England from Australia to see her grandchildren, who she can only adore from afar for the time being. Whilst she felt let down and naturally angry when John passed, essentially stopping her life in her tracks, how wonderful that she has found new happiness. Whilst never forgetting his great love Lorraine, Cousin Stephen has met someone new and continues to provide love and support to his four children, Joanne, Matthew, Dominic, and Richard. Through these boys, and Angela, the Kirby name survives and creates new posterity. I hope to see or hear from Denise again.

Like us, our friends can look to the future, however uncertain. Mark and Jonathan continue to work selflessly for the NHS and are moving to Leeds to start a new life nearer to their families. Beth and Alex are now first-time homeowners and planning their future life together. I will be going to their wedding whenever they get round to planning it. Jennifer and Gordon keep busy; their son, George, has a new girlfriend. Geraldine and Richard delight in their retirement and grandparent duties for Joanne's and Vicky's children. Jean soldiers on, the last of her generation still standing. Fran and Aaron are surviving and enjoying a happy life in the country with their four children. Martin and Peter are continuing to cultivate their gardening business as best they can in the current circumstances, and they will be down to create an oasis for us here in Deal as soon as things return to normal. My friend John hopes to resume his British Airways job flying to distant realms again one day, if he can. I miss seeing them all, along with Lee, Claudine, Lauren, Tom, and Sam and Mark from Harber Hair in London. And Penny and Victor in Mexico who have always been so generous and kind, and their sons Tram and Wally in New York. I hope Katie is well. Nolan is good, delighting in becoming an uncle to Tia's daughter, and since dog walking is now out, he is developing his new business venture, which I know will be a great success. Mum and Dad met many of my friends. Beth never had the chance to meet them but wanted to. And they would have liked Nolan had they been able to know him better. They were pleased I had found someone who makes me happy—and we are.

I'm looking forward to building a life with new friends along with the old ones here on the coast in Deal, keeping our bolthole in London too so I can be reminded of my roots. Wherever I am, and not knowing what might come along in the future, I plan to become an eccentric I think. Mum and Dad will join me in the garden soon, along with the robins who will come and find us, so we will all be together again.

And I have written this. If nothing else, it has been a way for me to document the recent events that have affected me so significantly, trying to record what I can of the feelings, thoughts, and recollections that I have.

It will be something for me to read and revisit as the years go by when the events chronicled here become more distant. But none of it will be forgotten. Hopefully it will be the good memories, the majority, that will be remembered most.

Above all, this has been written for Mum and Dad. I miss you.

And yesterday, on his first birthday, Frankie went into the sea for the first time.

Lightning Source UK Ltd.
Milton Keynes UK
UKHW042021091120
373076UK00003B/272